BRITISH

Weight
Watchers

COOKERY BOOK

by Bernice Weston

D1477290

Elm Tree Books in association with
Hamish Hamilton and Weight
Watchers Publications Ltd.

*My own weight loss came about through group
activity and co-operation. So did this book.
To Beryl Townsend, Barbara Hardwick,
Penny MacDermid, Ray Meylan and
Rita Grosvenor — my gratitude and appreciation
for their guidance and their long labours.*

*To British Weight Watchers —
my applause for the originality and their creative
contributions to this book.*

*To Leslie Levonton, our Staff at Windsor
and all of our Supervisors, Lecturers,
Clerks and Weighers who day and night carry
the Weight Watchers message of hope and success
to all fat people everywhere — my thanks.*

*To Jean Nidetch, my formerly-fat Fairy Godmother,
whose sparks of genius and humanity
are the source from which all good things come —
my reverence and devotion.*

**And to Richard Weston,
tenacious taster, galloping gourmet,
protective partner, kind counsellor —
my favourite cook — and only Husband
— my Love.**

First published in Great Britain
by Elm Tree Books in association with
Hamish Hamilton Ltd., 90 Great Russell
Street, London W.C.1, and Weight
Watchers Publications Ltd., 2, Thames
Street, Windsor, Berkshire, 1970

Second Impression, January 1971

Copyright © 1970 by Bernice Weston
All rights reserved

SBN 241 01987 7

Book layout and decorations by
Artes Graphicae Limited, London, England

Photographs by Angel Studio

Front cover dining chairs and table by G-Plan

Printed in Great Britain by
Sir Joseph Causton & Sons Ltd.,
Eastleigh, Hampshire

4

CONTENTS

INTRODUCTION

Welcome to dinner. On the front cover I appear with the meal I would serve you if you could be my guest. Colourful, original and tasty, it should tempt you to accept my invitation to eat the kind of food already sampled by hundreds of thousands of British Weight Watchers.

Eating to become or to keep slim need not be punishment — it can be a positive pleasure. We Weight Watchers enjoy sauces, snacks, thick soups, casseroles, roasts, even tempting puddings, as well as many other exciting dishes which we are pleased to share with you.

If this book interests you, you are either "involved" with food, anxious to keep your slim form, concerned about your weight or the weight of someone who is dear to you. You are right to be interested, anxious and concerned — overweight is a worry, in many instances a killer.

I know exactly what it means to be fat. Most of my life I was overweight. At 20 I weighed 10 st. 8 lb. and as a lass of 5 ft. 2 ins. with a small frame, I looked like a short fat pear. I shared a flat once with three skinny models — nice girls — good friends. One day I overheard them discussing a blind date for me. "If only we could introduce her sitting down" said one, "then he wouldn't get the full impact of her and he might get to like her for what she says and what she is."
Thanks to Weight Watchers I am now almost

as thin as they were, but inside my 8 st. 4 lb. frame remains the fat girl — always waiting to reassert herself. That is why I am still and must always be a member of Weight Watchers.
I first heard about Weight Watchers four years ago when I went on a visit to America with my husband Richard, like me a lawyer and — like me — fat. We sought the "latest thing" in dieting from my brother, a heart specialist in Miami, who surprised us by saying, "I send my overweight patients to Weight Watchers. Many of them are alive today because Weight Watchers works, its Programme and group therapy classes makes them and keeps them slim."

Richard and I had been dieting for as long as we could remember. We had tried everything — diets, pills, injections, health farms, slimming machines — but had never found a real solution. Every time we stopped a diet or a course of treatment, we got fat again. At first the whole group therapy idea sounded like a gimmick. But we had tried everything else — why not this? So we joined and attended Weight Watchers classes. The meetings were interesting and fun and we followed their Programme of Eating. We actually lost weight without ever feeling hungry, bored, depressed or deprived, in fact our great complaint was that we had too much to eat. We felt better, looked better and, for the first time in many years, we actually felt healthy.

But losing weight wasn't what mattered, we had done it before — many times before. What counted was staying slim. Now three and a half years later I am still 8 st. 4 lb. I have been slim for the longest period of my adult life and as a Maintenance member of Weight Watchers I now eat chocolates and drink spirits and can have almost any food, however fattening.

Could what had worked for us, as well as for hundreds of thousands of American men, women and children, work as well for the fat people in Britain? At first we were not certain. But our own need to continue to attend Weight Watchers classes made us think we should at least try, and in February 1967 Richard and I opened the first British Weight Watchers class near our home in Datchet, Buckinghamshire. Today there are hundreds of weekly Weight Watchers classes all over Britain.

Why does Weight Watchers work? Firstly, it is not a diet which is only the short term answer to the lifetime problem of overweight. Bananas and milk will get you thin, so will starvation. But how long can you and will you be willing to survive like that?

Fat is not caused by the need to eat, but by the compulsion to eat incorrect quantities of those foods which make you fat. So Weight Watchers changes those bad eating habits and replaces them with a new way of eating which is taught and presented in the Weight Watchers Programme of Eating.

Fat people are not self-indulgent gluttons who must be punished with punishing diets. They are sick people, as permanently diseased as the diabetic or the man with heart disease. Thus the treatment itself must be lifelong, and it must be acceptable for a long term. To enable people to keep slim, they must feel non-deprived, non-bored and normal for the rest of their lives. Otherwise they could not live with the treatment or with themselves.

This Programme consists of normal foods only — meat, fish, poultry, cheese, eggs, fruit,

vegetables, milk and bread. There are no slimming foods allowed on the Programme. Thus normal food which you must eat can be eaten in restaurants, in other people's homes, at parties, at banquets, on holiday — without the necessity of anyone ever knowing you are slimming. For the first time fat people can concentrate on eating rather than starving — and can be sociable as well — and this they *can* live with.

The Programme, based on medical and scientific research carried out by the New York Board of Health Obesity Clinic, has been adapted and adjusted to our national tastes and habits. It is now a British way of eating. The Programme tells you what to eat, how much to eat and when to eat. Stick to the rules and it will work. Vary them to suit your convenience and appetite, and it won't. Do not worry about how much weight you have to lose, concern yourself only with getting through the next meal — legally. The success with which you meet that crisis will help you through the next meal and the next. Never skip a meal and always begin the day with breakfast. If you nibble compulsively, remain a compulsive nibbler without feeling guilty, but learn to nibble on what we call "unlimited foods" and make them interesting — enjoy a good munch. If you eat three properly balanced meals a day in generous quantities, you cannot possibly be hungry, and that is how the Programme works.

Getting fat people thin isn't simply a matter of giving each one the Programme of Eating and leaving them to it. The Programme is wonderful but the magic ingredient is the Weight Watchers classes. Most fat people cannot learn to re-educate their eating patterns on their own. They will cheat and fail, and they need the group to keep them going — especially when they have failed or had a temporary setback.

Weight Watchers brings together in weekly classes, men, women and children of all ages, from all walks of life, most of whom have only one thing in common — fat. Under the guidance of a trained and dedicated Lecturer, always a former fatty who has succeeded with Weight Watchers, they join together, encourage one another — sympathise, cheer and compete. Each classmate is a constant reminder of your own foibles and, because you share a mutual problem, it makes your own seem more bearable, while another member's success inspires you and makes your problem easier to solve.

At your first Weight Watchers class your ideal or "Goal" weight is assessed according to life assurance company tables.

Weight Watchers advises you to consult your doctor before starting on the Programme and, if you have any medical history or problem, we insist on your doctor's written permission. You attend weekly meetings and follow the Programme of Eating until you reach your "Goal" weight. Then you begin a Maintenance Programme which allows you to add to the Programme most of those foods and drinks which you have craved for and missed. After sixteen weeks as a member and on reaching "Goal" you become a free Lifetime Member who now attends only once-monthly classes.

Overweight can be as much as 12 stone or as little as 10 lb. — you never quite realise how uncomfortable every pound is until you lose it. That point was really brought home to one of our Weight Watchers the day her washing machine broke down in the middle of its washing cycle, leaving her with a mass of heavy, wet clothes. She and her husband huffed and puffed down to the Launderette where the half-washed clothes were put on the scales. They weighed 2 stone, her exact weight loss, weight which she had carried about year after dangerous, unhealthy year. To be slim is not only more healthy and more comfortable, a new shape often means a completely new outlook on life. Many men and women find that their lives, careers and marriages take on a whole new flavour.

At the start do not expect your family, or slim friends, to help you. In their eyes you are a born loser, always trying to slim, but always failing. When they see that you are in earnest, that you will not be tempted, that you are not cheating and eating in secret, they will help you. But they still will not want to suffer on your account.

And why should they suffer because you are fat? This is why the Weight Watchers Programme is so easy for women who have a family to consider as well as themselves. Weight Watchers food fits easily into a normal life and the everyday commitment of feeding a family.

There is no need for you to cook separate meals, one for you, one for them. You simply share the same meal but you eat more, or less, depending on what the Programme says. If your guests or family are having a fattening sauce, you remove your meat or fish from the casserole before adding the thickening. Then you indulge yourself in one of the delicious Weight Watchers sauces you have made up in bulk at the beginning of the week and which is now in the refrigerator ready for instant use. Weight Watchers frequently serve completely "legal" meals to their husbands, families and friends who never notice the difference except that they, too, feel better.

Many of the recipes in this book are prize-winning ones submitted by British Weight Watchers who used their ingenuity and imagination to create delicious alternatives to those recipes which used to make them fat. But don't expect these recipes alone to make you slim. Only regular attendance at Weight Watchers classes and following the complete Programme of Eating can do that. The purpose of this Weight Watchers Cook Book is to help Weight Watchers and their fat friends make food fun to cook and a joy to eat, and to show civilians — which is what I call skinnies — that our recipes are not only health-giving but every bit as exciting and inviting as the recipes in other cookery books. Preparing these recipes for ourselves and for you has been a labour of love. Thank you for joining us and "*Bon Appetit*".

Recipe Instructions

Weight Watchers – please read before preparing recipes

If you are preparing more than one course, check recipes carefully to ensure that you are not exceeding your meal time or daily allowance of limited foods.

Recipes marked **"Unlimited"** may be eaten in any quantity when and as often as desired.

All gelatine used must be unflavoured.

All tinned fish must be drained of oil before use.

One slice of bread shall be no more than one ounce in weight.

Dishes containing fish, meat or poultry: these when prepared according to the recipe will meet the exact Weight Watchers meal time allowances. However, it is still a very good idea to weigh your food after cooking.

The weights given for fish, meat or poultry in dinner recipes are the permitted allowance for ladies. The number of portions are indicated at either the top or foot of the recipe. Men must increase their dinner time allowance of fish, meat or poultry according to their requirements.

Note To Non-Weight Watchers

Daily allowances, limited and non-limited foods, and legal and illegal foods are fully explained in the Weight Watchers Programme of Eating which is available only to registered members of Weight Watchers. These recipes have been arranged according to meal time requirements (breakfast, lunch and dinner) and should not be interchanged or the daily balance will be interrupted.

BREAKFAST
AND QUICK SNACKS

9

Mid-Morning
Bouillon – unlimited

8 fl. oz. chicken stock made
from bouillon cube
Dried garlic flakes to taste
Few drops of lemon juice
Serves 1

Mix all ingredients. Serve very hot. This bouillon is very refreshing on summer days served chilled.

Egg Meringue Ring

1 slice bread
1 egg
Salt and pepper
Serves 1

Toast slice of bread. Break and separate egg. Whisk the egg white until very stiff, then season well. Spoon into a ring on slice of toast, drop yolk into the centre and bake in a fairly hot oven (375°F or Mark 5) for 5 to 8 minutes or until set.

Mushroom Cheese on Toast

1 lb. button mushrooms
Little skimmed milk
1 slice bread
1 oz. hard cheese, grated
Serves 1

Wash mushrooms and slice into non-stick frying pan. Add milk and simmer gently until cooked. Toast bread on both sides. Drain mushrooms from liquid; pile onto toast, sprinkle cheese over the top and grill until golden.

12

Mushroom Rarebit

1 oz. Cheddar cheese
2 medium sized mushrooms
1 slice bread
A little chopped parsley
Serves 1

Grate cheese and finely chop mushrooms. Mix both well together. Toast bread on one side only. Spread untoasted side with cheese/mushroom mixture taking care to cover bread completely. Grill briskly until golden and bubbly. Sprinkle with a little chopped parsley. Serve immediately with, if liked, Worcestershire sauce or mustard.

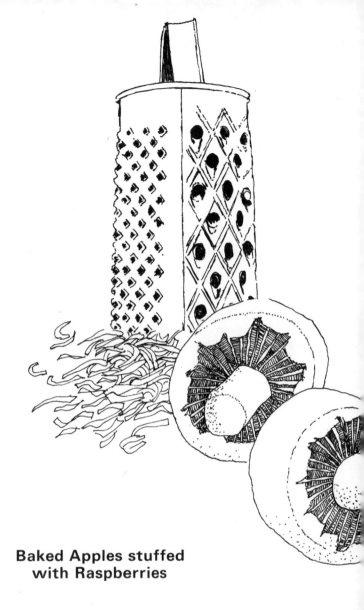

Morning Mushrooms

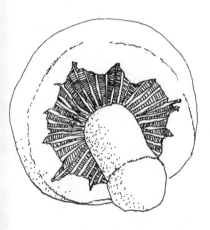

1½ fl. oz. tomato juice
4 medium mushrooms, chopped
1 egg
1 slice bread (toasted)
Serves 1

Simmer mushrooms in tomato juice in a small covered pan for 5 minutes. Add egg to the mixture, cover pan and cook gently for 3 – 4 minutes depending on whether you like a hard or soft egg. Serve on toast.

Baked Apples stuffed with Raspberries

4 medium sized cooking apples
8 oz. fresh or frozen raspberries
¼ teaspoon cinnamon
Artificial sweetener to taste
¼ pint water
Serves 4

Remove cores two thirds of way down each apple. With sharp knife, score line round each apple, about one third way down from top. Stand in shallow dish. Put water, sweetener and cinnamon into pan and bring to boil. Simmer one minute, then remove from the heat. Add whole raspberries and stuff centres of apples with this mixture. Pour remainder over top. Cover with foil and bake in centre of moderate oven (350°F or Mark 4) for 45 minutes or until apples are tender.

See Photograph on Pages 10 and 11.

Honeydew Melon Salad

1 small honeydew melon
¼ cucumber
4 stalks celery, thinly sliced
1 fresh pineapple
Artificial liquid sweetener to taste
1 red-skinned eating apple, diced
2 fl. oz. unsweetened orange juice
To decorate: fresh mint leaves
Serves 3

Cut melon in half and, with a scoop, shape flesh into balls. Place melon shell to one side. Shape the cucumber flesh into balls and combine with the celery, pineapple and eating apple. Pour over the orange juice and add liquid sweetener to taste. Pile mixture into melon shell and decorate with fresh mint leaves before serving.

Below: Apple Medley

Cottage Cucumber Toast

1 slice bread

1 oz. cottage cheese

Approx. 12 thin slices cucumber

½ oz. grated hard cheese

Garlic salt

Serves 1

Toast bread on one side and lightly on the other. Spread light side with cottage cheese, then arrange cucumber slices on top. Shred or grate the hard cheese over the cucumber and sprinkle generously with garlic salt. Grill briskly until golden and bubbly.

Apple Medley

1 red-skinned eating apple

Low calorie squash (1 tablespoon diluted with ¼ pint water)

1 slice white or brown bread

2 oz. cottage cheese

¼ teaspoon cinnamon

Serves 1

Core and slice the apple. Put into flameproof dish with the squash. Poach in centre of moderate oven (350°F or Mark 4) until tender — about 15 – 20 minutes. Toast bread on one side only. Spread untoasted side with cheese and arrange poached apple slices on top. Sprinkle with cinnamon and baste with a little juice remaining in the dish. Lightly brown under grill.

Crunchy Celery Boats

2 oz. cottage cheese
2 sticks celery
3 lettuce leaves
1 slice bread
Paprika
Serves 1

Wash celery and cut into 1-inch lengths. Fill each piece with cottage cheese, sprinkle with paprika. Arrange lettuce on a plate and on it place the stuffed celery pieces in a circle. Toast bread and cut into fingers.

Gingered Pineapple

1 fresh pineapple
1 bottle low-calorie ginger ale
Cinnamon and artificial sweetener to taste
Serves 4

Cut pineapple into quarters. Remove shell and slice. Place in baking dish with ginger ale. Sprinkle with cinnamon and sweetener. Bake in a moderate oven (350°F or Mark 4) for approximately 30 minutes. Baste occasionally.

LUNCH

Soups and Hors d' Oeuvres
Weight Watchers All-In-Soup — unlimited/**20**
Chinese Style Cabbage Soup — unlimited/**20**
Lemon Chicken Soup — unlimited/**21**
Soup Piquant — unlimited/**21**
Winter Soup — unlimited/**21**
Thick Tomato Soup — unlimited/**21**
Country Soup — unlimited/**23**
Hungarian Thick Soup — unlimited/**23**
Cauliflower and Tomato Soup — unlimited/**23**
Unlimited Glory — unlimited/**24**
Spinach Cocktail — unlimited/**24**
Piquant Celery Sticks — unlimited/**24**
Cucumber Mould — unlimited/**24**
Summer Salad Aspic — unlimited/**25**
Polish Mushrooms — unlimited/**25**
Tomato Vegetable Aspic — unlimited/**25**
Vegetable Appetizer — unlimited/**25**

Main Dishes
Sole in Breadcrumbs/**28**
Scrambled Fish Toasts/**28**
Windsor Castle Galantine/**29**
Spicy Baked Fish/**29**
Shrimp Chow Mein/**30**
Salmon Soufflé/**30**
Salmon Piquant/**31**
Creamed Salmon/**31**
Grilled Tuna Roll/**31**
Sage and Onion Tuna/**31**
Tuna Cheese Spread/**32**
Tuna Salad in Orange Cup/**32**
Fish Pâté/**32**
Mock Bolognaise/**32**
Beefburgers/**33**
Steak and Mushroom Pie/**33**
Minced Liver/**33**

Weight Watchers All-In-Soup
— unlimited

*2 heaped tablespoons shredded
white cabbage*

1 stick celery, chopped

1 small or $\frac{1}{2}$ medium cauliflower, chopped

$1\frac{1}{2}$ pints water

2 oz. courgettes

1 oz. mushrooms, chopped

1 bayleaf

$\frac{1}{2}$ level teaspoon dried dill

1 clove garlic, crushed (optional)

1 beef stock cube

Salt

Serves 4

Put all the ingredients except the stock in a saucepan and bring to the boil. Cover pan and simmer gently for about 45 minutes until all the vegetables are soft. Remove bayleaf. Add stock cube and heat to dissolve. Adjust seasoning and serve piping hot either with the vegetables as they are or blend in the liquidizer and serve smooth.

Chinese Style Cabbage Soup
— unlimited

For each person allow:

$\frac{1}{4}$ pint water

6 tablespoons tomato juice

1 to 3 dessertspoons soy sauce

Salt and pepper

$\frac{1}{2}$ lb. white cabbage, chopped

Put water, tomato juice, soy sauce, salt and pepper into a saucepan. Add cabbage and cook slowly for 10 to 15 minutes.

Lemon Chicken Soup – unlimited

1 chicken stock cube
$\frac{3}{4}$ pint hot water
2 oz. mushrooms
1 tablespoon chopped parsley
2 teaspoons fresh lemon juice
Serves 2

Dissolve chicken stock cube in hot water. Wash mushrooms, slice thinly and add to stock with parsley. Simmer for a few minutes until mushrooms are tender. Take off heat and stir in lemon juice.

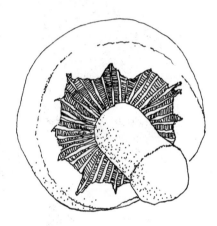

Soup Piquant – unlimited

14 fl. oz. tomato juice
4 oz. frozen sliced runner beans
4 oz. chopped mushrooms
2 heaped teaspoons dried onion flakes
1 large chopped gherkin
A few drops Worcestershire sauce, to taste
$\frac{1}{4}$ teaspoon salt
Freshly ground black pepper, to taste
Serves 3 – 4

Put tomato juice into saucepan with an equal amount of water. While liquid is boiling, lower heat and add all remaining ingredients. Simmer gently for 10 minutes.

Winter Soup – unlimited

$\frac{1}{2}$ pint tomato juice
$\frac{1}{2}$ beef bouillon cube
1 teaspoon chopped mint
2 teaspoons chopped parsley
Salt and pepper
Dash of Worcestershire sauce
Artificial liquid sweetener to equal
2 teaspoons sugar
4 oz. cabbage, finely shredded
2 stalks celery, finely sliced
2 bunches watercress, chopped
$\frac{1}{4}$ box mustard and cress, chopped
Serves 2

Put first seven ingredients into a saucepan and bring to the boil. Add rest of ingredients; again bring to the boil; cover pan and simmer for 10 – 15 minutes until vegetables are tender-crisp. Adjust seasonings and serve as a very hearty soup or thin down with water if preferred.

Thick Tomato Soup – unlimited

2 chicken stock cubes
4 fl. oz. hot water
12 fl. oz. tomato juice
2 teaspoons dried onion flakes
1 lb. marrow, peeled, cored and diced
Pepper
Few drops artificial sweetener (if liked)
Serves 2 – 3

Dissolve the stock cubes in hot water, add rest of ingredients, except pepper and sweetener, and bring to the boil. Cover pan and simmer gently until marrow is tender – about 20 minutes. Place in blender until smooth. Return to pan and season with pepper and liquid sweetener if necessary. Serve piping hot.

Country Soup –
unlimited

22

Hungarian Thick Soup
— unlimited

1 tin (1 lb. 3 oz.) celery hearts, drained

4 oz. button mushrooms, sliced

½ pint water

2 teaspoons paprika

¼ teaspoon dried tarragon

Salt and pepper

Serves 4

Liquidize the celery hearts or mash well with a fork. Place in a saucepan with the other ingredients. Bring to the boil, cover pan and simmer gently for 10 – 15 minutes. Adjust seasonings and serve.

Cauliflower and Tomato Soup
— unlimited

1 small cauliflower using outside leaves

½ pint tomato juice

¾ pint water

1 chicken stock cube

Salt and pepper

¼ lb. button mushrooms, sliced

1 level teaspoon basil

1 tablespoon chopped parsley

Serves 4

Country Soup — unlimited

1 teaspoonful dried onion flakes

*¼ pint chicken stock made
from bouillon cube*

6 tablespoons tomato juice

3 to 4 mushrooms, chopped

Seasoning

Serves 1

Wash cauliflower and cut into small pieces. Put in a pan with tomato juice, water and stock cube. Bring to the boil, cover and simmer until tender — about 15 minutes. Cool slightly and put into blender with seasonings and mushrooms. Blend till smooth. Add basil and return to the pan, bring to the boil, simmer for 3 minutes, adjust seasonings and just before serving stir in the parsley. If you want a creamed soup add a heaped teaspoon skimmed milk powder to serving of soup.

Simmer onion flakes in chicken stock until soft. Add rest of ingredients and simmer for 10 minutes.

Unlimited Glory – unlimited

1 medium cauliflower

2 celery stalks, chopped

$\frac{1}{2}$ green pepper, diced

1 teaspoon parsley flakes

$\frac{1}{2}$ teaspoon lemon juice

1 teaspoon salt

$\frac{1}{2}$ teaspoon Worcestershire sauce

1 pickled cucumber, chopped

1 tablespoon dried onion flakes

$\frac{1}{2}$ teaspoon Aromat

1 teaspoon liquid sugar substitute

1 tablespoon prepared mustard

3-4 radishes, sliced

Serves 2 – 3

Boil cauliflower with onion flakes for 15 minutes. Drain and chop. Combine thoroughly with all the remaining ingredients and chill before serving.

Spinach Cocktail – unlimited

$\frac{1}{2}$ pint tomato juice

$\frac{1}{2}$ teaspoon salt

Generous pinch garlic powder

2 spinach leaves

1 oz. spinach, blanched and shredded

7 oz. cauliflower florets

1 tablespoon lemon juice

$\frac{1}{2}$ tablespoon grated horseradish

Serves 2

Combine tomato juice, salt and garlic powder. Cook uncovered over medium heat until tomato juice is reduced by half. Chill. Place a spinach leaf in each of 2 large wine goblets or small bowls. Place half shredded spinach in each and fill glasses with cauliflower florets and mushrooms. Combine reduced tomato juice, lemon juice and horseradish and pour over cocktail.

24

Piquant Celery Sticks – unlimited

1 lb. celery

2 tablespoons soy sauce

1 tablespoon vinegar

Artificial sweetener to taste

1 teaspoon Aromat

Serves 4 – 6

Cut celery into approx. 1-inch lengths. Parboil in boiling water for 2 minutes. Rinse with cold water. Drain and cool 5 minutes. Add rest of ingredients. Chill $\frac{1}{2}$ hour in refrigerator before serving.

Cucumber Mould – unlimited

4 envelopes gelatine

$\frac{3}{4}$ pint chicken stock, hot

$2\frac{1}{4}$ pints cold water

3 tablespoons lemon juice

2 tablespoons cider vinegar

Pinch salt

2/3 drops green food colouring

$\frac{1}{2}$ cucumber, sliced

$\frac{1}{2}$ cucumber, diced

1 bunch radishes, sliced

Green salad selection – lettuce, chicory, watercress, mustard and cress

Radish roses for garnish

Serves 6

Dissolve gelatine in hot stock. Stir in cold water, lemon juice, vinegar, salt and food colouring. Chill until slightly thickened. Spoon a $\frac{1}{2}$" layer of gelatine mixture into $3\frac{1}{2}$ pint mould. Overlap and press cucumber slices into gelatine. Chill until firm. Fold diced cucumber and radishes into remaining gelatine and pour gently on top of first layer. Chill until completely firm. Unmould on top of green salad and garnish with radish roses.

Summer Salad Aspic — unlimited

$\frac{3}{4}$ pint water

6 tablespoons cider vinegar

$\frac{3}{4}$ teaspoon liquid sweetener

2 tablespoons lemon juice

$\frac{1}{2}$ level teaspoon garlic salt

Black pepper

2 $\frac{1}{2}$-oz. packets powdered gelatine

1 cucumber, peeled and grated

2 sticks celery or 1 head chicory, finely sliced

1 teaspoon chopped parsley

8 oz. cabbage, finely shredded

$\frac{1}{2}$ green pepper, deseeded and chopped

2 caps tinned peppers, chopped

Serves 4

Combine $\frac{1}{2}$ pint water, vinegar, sweetener, lemon juice, garlic salt and pepper. Dissolve gelatine in remaining water in a basin over a pan of hot water, then add to final liquid. Combine the rest of the ingredients and add the liquid. Mix thoroughly and turn into a mould; chill until set.

Polish Mushrooms — unlimited

$\frac{1}{2}$ lb. small mushrooms

1 teaspoon salt

$\frac{1}{4}$ pint cider vinegar

6 peppercorns

$\frac{1}{4}$ teaspoon dried onion flakes

1 sprig parsley

1 bay leaf

3 celery leaves

Serves 1—2

Wash mushrooms, trim stems and set aside. Meanwhile, combine all other ingredients and boil for 10 minutes. Pour over drained mushrooms and let cool. When cool, put in tightly covered jar and shake. Refrigerate for at least 24 hours before using. Drain liquid before serving.

Tomato Vegetable Aspic — unlimited

$\frac{3}{4}$ pint tomato juice

1 envelope gelatine

1 $\frac{1}{2}$ teaspoons lemon juice

$\frac{1}{2}$ teaspoon dried onion flakes

$\frac{1}{2}$ teaspoon Worcestershire sauce

$\frac{1}{4}$ teaspoon salt

2 stalks celery, finely diced

$\frac{1}{3}$ cucumber, diced

Lettuce

Serves 4

Soften gelatine in 3 tablespoons of the tomato juice. Heat remaining juice until boiling, then remove from the heat. Add the softened gelatine and stir until dissolved. Add seasonings. Chill until partially set before adding the diced vegetables. Spoon into one large mould or four individual moulds and chill until firm. Unmould onto lettuce and garnish with cucumber curls, made from peel.

Vegetable Appetizer — unlimited

$\frac{1}{2}$ lb. courgettes, topped and tailed and cut into rings

$\frac{1}{2}$ teaspoon salt

Freshly ground black pepper

1 red pepper

$\frac{1}{2}$ cucumber

Chopped parsley

1 envelope gelatine

$\frac{1}{2}$ pint tomato juice

1 teaspoon Worcestershire sauce

Serves 4—5

Cook the courgettes until tender in a little salted water, about 10 minutes. Drain and arrange in a large dish or individual dishes. Season well. Slice pepper and cucumber and arrange on top of courgettes. Sprinkle with chopped parsley. Dissolve gelatine in hot water, before adding to the tomato juice. Stir in the Worcestershire sauce and pour over vegetables. Chill until set.

Spinach Cocktail – unlimited

Opposite: Vegetable Appetizer – unlimited

Tomato Vegetable Aspic – unlimited

26

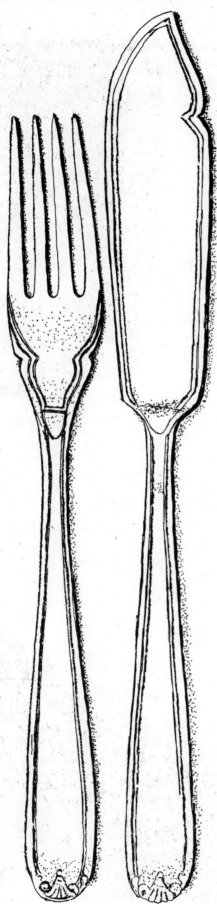

Sole in Breadcrumbs

¼ pint skimmed milk
1 teaspoon salt
½ teaspoon Worcestershire sauce
2 teaspoons dried onion flakes
4 slices bread (crumb in liquidizer)
¼ teaspoon dry mustard
½ teaspoon paprika
1½ lb. sole fillets
Serves 4

Mix milk, salt, Worcestershire sauce and onion flakes in a bowl. Combine breadcrumbs, mustard and paprika on a piece of greaseproof paper. Dip fish in milk mixture and then in crumb mixture (coat both sides). Place in shallow baking pan. Bake in a fairly hot oven (400°F or Gas Mark 6) for 20 minutes or until fish flakes easily with fork.

Scrambled Fish Toasts

4 oz. cooked white fish
4 tablespoons skimmed milk
2 eggs
Salt and pepper
Good pinch cayenne pepper
2 slices toast
Chopped parsley
Serves 2

Flake the fish removing any skin and bones and heat gently in 2 tablespoons milk. Beat eggs, remaining milk, salt, pepper and cayenne pepper together and cook gently in a non-stick pan, stirring all the time, until thick. Beat in the fish. Cut hot toast into 6 fingers and pile the fish scramble on top. Sprinkle with chopped parsley and serve.

Windsor Castle Galantine

6 oz. raw cod fillet, skinned

2 level teaspoons dried onion flakes

2 level teaspoons dried parsley flakes

$\frac{1}{4}$ level teaspoon oregano

1 tablespoon wine vinegar

1 chicken stock cube

4 fl. oz. hot water

Salt and pepper

$\frac{1}{2}$ oz. packet powdered gelatine

Serves 1

Put all the ingredients except the gelatine into a pan and bring to the boil. Cover pan and simmer very gently for about 10 minutes until fish is tender. Mash the fish into the cooking liquid. Dissolve gelatine in 3 tablespoons water in a basin over a pan of hot water, then stir into the fish mixture. Pour into a dish and put in a cold place until set. Turn out onto a bed of lettuce and serve.

Spicy Baked Fish

$\frac{1}{2}$ teaspoon paprika

$\frac{1}{2}$ teaspoon onion powder

$\frac{1}{2}$ teaspoon garlic powder

$\frac{1}{2}$ teaspoon salt

$\frac{1}{2}$ teaspoon pepper

$\frac{1}{2}$ teaspoon Aromat

12 oz. halibut, cod or haddock fillets

Serves 2

Cover base of a shallow baking dish with foil. Combine all ingredients except fish. Sprinkle half over foil. Place fish on top. Sprinkle with remaining seasonings. Grill about 3 inches from source of heat for 10 minutes or until fish flakes easily with fork. Turn once during grilling.

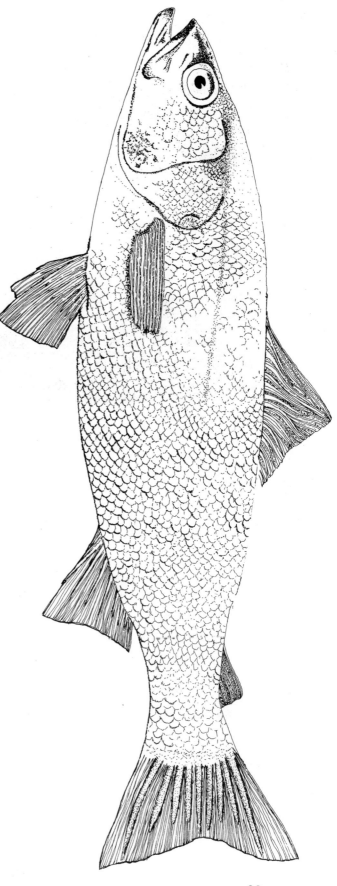

29

Shrimp Chow Mein

Shrimp Chow Mein

1 green pepper, seeded and finely sliced

3 oz. button mushrooms, finely sliced (optional)

2 stalks celery, finely sliced

2 level teaspoons dried onion flakes

12 fl. oz. tomato juice

Salt and pepper

1 tablespoon soy sauce

1 teaspoon lemon juice

7 oz. bean sprouts, drained

8 oz. tinned shrimps, drained

Serves 2

Put all ingredients in a saucepan, except bean sprouts and shrimps. Bring to the boil, cover and simmer for 10 minutes. Add bean sprouts and shrimps and heat through for about 3 minutes. Adjust seasonings and serve.

30

Salmon Soufflé

2 eggs, separated

$\frac{1}{4}$ pint skimmed milk

2 slices day old bread (without crusts)

4 oz. tinned salmon, drained

$\frac{1}{4}$ level teaspoon dried dill

Salt and pepper

1 teaspoon chopped parsley

Serves 2

Beat egg yolks into milk and put into a double saucepan with the dried bread. Cook gently until thick, stirring all the time (do not allow to boil). Remove from the heat. Mash salmon and add to the mixture with dill, seasoning and parsley. Mix thoroughly. Whisk egg whites until stiff and fold carefully into the salmon mixture. Put into an ovenproof dish and stand in a roasting tin containing 1 inch water. Cook at 375°F or Mark 5 for 40 – 45 minutes until risen and golden brown.

Salmon Piquant

1 tablespoon dried onion flakes

¼ teaspoon garlic powder

¼ teaspoon Tabasco

8 oz. tinned salmon, flaked

8 fl. oz. tomato juice

1 tablespoon capers

2 slices toast

Serves 2

Add onion flakes, garlic powder, and Tabasco to tomato juice. Simmer, uncovered, until tomato juice is reduced by half. Stir in salmon and capers. Cook an additional 4 minutes. Divide mixture in half. Serve each over 1 slice of toast.

Grilled Tuna Roll

2 oz. tinned tuna fish, flaked

1 hardboiled egg, chopped

1 oz. mushrooms, finely chopped

Salt and pepper

2 teaspoons Worcestershire sauce

1 thin slice bread without crusts

Lettuce, cucumber, radishes, lemon slices and watercress for garnish

Serves 1

Mash the tuna with egg, mushrooms, seasonings and Worcestershire sauce. Heat gently in a non-stick pan. Spread mixture on to the bread, roll up carefully, and secure with 2 cocktail sticks. Score top in two places, place on a piece of foil and put under a medium grill until golden brown. Serve on a bed of lettuce and watercress and garnish with cucumber, radishes and sliced lemon.

Sage and Onion Tuna

1 slice bread

4 oz. tinned tuna

½ teaspoon dried sage (or to taste)

¼ pint plus 4 tablespoons water

½ chicken stock cube

1 large celery stalk, with leaves, chopped

Dash of black pepper

1 teaspoon dried onion flakes

Serves 1

Creamed Salmon

8 oz. tinned salmon

1 oz. dried skimmed milk

3 tablespoons water

1 tablespoon chopped capers

1 teaspoon dried onion flakes
(soaked 10 minutes in hot water and drained)

2 oz. wholemeal breadcrumbs

Serves 2

Flake salmon and combine with remaining ingredients except breadcrumbs. Transfer to shallow heatproof dish. Sprinkle with breadcrumbs and cook in moderate oven (350°F or Mark 4) for 20 to 30 minutes or until crisp on top. Serve with lemon wedges and a green salad.

Cut bread into small cubes. Combine with tuna and sage in mixing bowl. In saucepan, combine all remaining ingredients. Simmer over medium heat until celery is tender. Add to tuna mixture. (Mixture should be moist and cling together; add 1 or 2 tablespoons water if necessary). Transfer to heatproof dish and bake in a moderate oven (350°F or Mark 4) for about 1 hour or until golden.

Tuna Cheese Spread

2 oz. tinned tuna
1 tablespoon liquid skimmed milk
1 slice bread
1 oz. Cheddar cheese
Serves 1

Mix tuna with milk. Spread over bread. Cover with cheese and grill until cheese melts.

Fish Pâté

4 oz. tinned tuna or salmon
1 teaspoon dried onion flakes
1 stalk celery, diced
1 tablespoon pickled red cabbage
1 or 2 teaspoons mustard
Salt and pepper
1 slice bread, toasted
Serves 1

Combine all ingredients, except bread, and spread on toast.

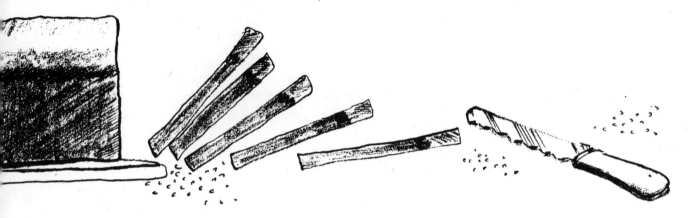

Tuna Salad in Orange Cup

2 large oranges
8 oz. tinned tuna, flaked
2 celery stalks, thinly sliced
½ tablespoon Worcestershire sauce
2 tablespoons chopped cucumber
1 tablespoon tinned red pepper, chopped
1 tablespoon tomato juice
Salt
Freshly ground black pepper
Parsley for garnish
Serves 2

Cut top off both oranges about one third of the way down. (Scallop edge if desired.) Scoop out flesh and cut up. Combine with remaining ingredients, then spoon into hollowed-out orange-shells. Top with the orange cap, and a sprig of parsley.

Mock Bolognaise

12 oz. tomato juice
¼ teaspoon oregano leaves
1 bay leaf
¼ teaspoon garlic salt
Artificial sweetener to equal
1 tablespoon sugar
1 tin bean sprouts, well drained
8 oz. cooked beef or lamb, minced
Parsley
Serves 2

Combine the tomato juice, oregano, bay leaf, garlic salt and sweetener in saucepan. Add meat and simmer, covered, for 25 minutes. Remove bay leaf. Heat through bean sprouts, strain, and place on a serving dish. Pour bolognaise over and decorate with parsley sprigs.

Beefburgers

6 oz. lean minced beef
1 slice bread, soaked in water
½ teaspoon prepared mustard
Onion, salt and pepper to taste
Pinch of mixed sweet herbs
Serves 1

Combine beef with bread (first squeezed dry) and all remaining ingredients. Shape into two cakes, each ½-inch in thickness. Grill about 6 minutes, turning frequently. Serve with a green salad.

Steak and Mushroom Pie

18 oz. chuck steak
1 beef stock cube
¾ pint tomato juice
Salt and pepper
Dash of Worcestershire sauce
9 oz. button mushrooms
3 oz. white breadcrumbs
Serves 3

Cut steak into small cubes and put into a pan with stock cube, ½ pint tomato juice, salt, pepper and Worcestershire sauce. Bring to the boil, cover and simmer very gently for about 1½ hours until meat is tender. Cool completely (preferably overnight). Skim off fat. Add the remaining ¼ pint tomato juice and the mushrooms and bring to the boil. Cover and simmer for 30 minutes. Transfer to an individual ovenproof dish and cover with bread-crumbs. Put under a moderate grill for about 5 minutes until crumbs are a golden brown crust.

Minced Liver

4 oz. cooked liver, minced
1 oz. white breadcrumbs
2 level teaspoons dried sage
Salt and pepper
2 level teaspoons dried onion flakes
7 fl. oz. water
½ beef bouillon cube
Chopped parsley
Serves 1

Mix together liver, breadcrumbs, sage, salt, pepper and onion flakes. Dissolve beef bouillon cube in water in a pan and bring to the boil. Add the other ingredients, mix well and simmer, covered, for about 10 minutes. Arrange on a plate and garnish with chopped parsley before serving.

Caribbean Casserole

2 large green peppers
2 hardboiled eggs, chopped
4 oz. crab meat
½ pint tomato juice
1 level teaspoon dried onion flakes
Salt and pepper
¼ lb. button mushrooms, sliced
1 stick celery, chopped
Good dash Worcestershire sauce
Serves 2

Cut tops off peppers and remove seeds. Blanch in boiling water for 5 minutes. Drain. Mix together chopped eggs, crab meat, 3 tablespoons tomato juice, onion flakes, salt and pepper and stuff peppers with this mixture. Put rest of tomato juice, salt and pepper, sliced mushrooms and chopped celery into a pan and bring to the boil. Add Worcestershire sauce. Place stuffed peppers in ovenproof dish and pour sauce around them. Cover casserole and cook at 400°F or Mark 6 for about 40 minutes until peppers are tender.

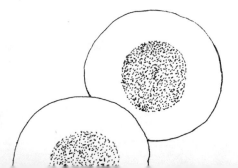

**Tuna Salad in
Orange Cup**

Liver Pâté and Mushroom Toast

12 oz. liver

$\frac{1}{4}$ pint stock

Salt and pepper

2 teaspoons Worcestershire sauce

$\frac{1}{2}$ teaspoon made mustard

2 tablespoons lemon juice

4 oz. button mushrooms

2 slices toast

Strips of green pepper and watercress
to garnish

Serves 2

**Veal and
Egg Salad**

Put liver into saucepan with stock and salt and
pepper to taste. Cook, covered, until tender.
Remove from pan, cut into dice and put into
liquidizer with Worcestershire sauce, mustard and
lemon juice. Blend until smooth and then add
sufficient stock to give a soft paste. Season to
taste. Spread on to toast, then top with mushrooms
which have been either boiled or "fried" in non-
stick pan. Place under pre-heated grill for 1 minute
then garnish with pepper and watercress.

34

Veal with Egg Croûtons

⅓ pint chicken stock,
made from bouillon cube

2 oz. cooked diced veal

1 egg

1 slice bread, cut into large dice

Pepper

Serves 1

Combine stock and veal. Bring to boil. Reduce heat and simmer. Meanwhile, beat egg. With fork, dip bread cubes into beaten egg. Leave to soak for a few minutes until egg is absorbed. Drop into simmering stock with veal and cook 4 minutes or until egg is set. Sprinkle with pepper.

Chicken Rissoles

2 oz. mushrooms, finely chopped

2 level teaspoons dried onion flakes

4 tablespoons skimmed milk

4 oz. cooked chicken, minced

1 oz. white breadcrumbs

Salt and pepper

Pinch of nutmeg

½ level teaspoonful skimmed
milk powder

Serves 1

Put mushrooms, onion flakes and milk in a small pan and simmer very gently for about 5 minutes. Mix chicken, breadcrumbs, salt, pepper and nutmeg together. Add mushroom mixture and bind together adding a little more milk if necessary. Form into 4 cakes and sprinkle with the milk powder. Put under a moderate grill for about 5 minutes, turning once.

**Cheesy Chicken and
Asparagus Salad**

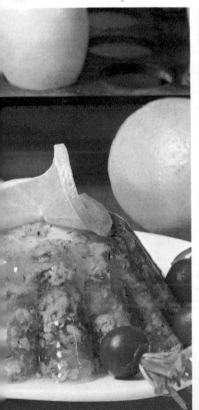

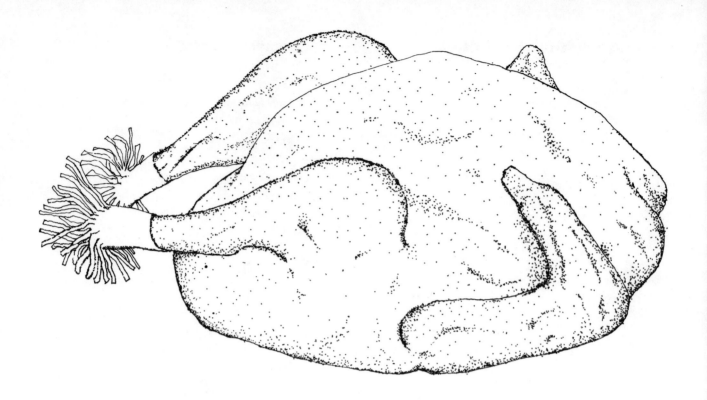

Veal and Egg Salad

$\frac{1}{2}$ stock cube

2 teaspoons powdered gelatine

$\frac{1}{2}$ pint hot water

$\frac{1}{2}$ teaspoon mixed dried herbs

$\frac{1}{2}$ teaspoon lemon juice

2 oz. cooked minced veal

Salt

Freshly ground black pepper

Green colouring

1 hard boiled egg

Watercress

Few chicory leaves and radishes for garnish

Serves 1

Chicken Curry

4 oz. cooked chicken

2 oz. mushrooms sliced

$\frac{1}{4}$ pint tomato juice

$\frac{1}{2}$ teaspoon Worcestershire sauce

$\frac{1}{8}$ teaspoon garlic salt

$\frac{1}{4}$ teaspoon salt

2 – 3 level teaspoons curry powder
(according to taste)

$\frac{1}{2}$ green pepper

$\frac{1}{2}$ red apple

4 oz. cauliflower, boiled

1 slice toast

Serves 1

Dissolve stock cube and gelatine in the hot water. Add herbs and lemon juice and green colouring. Put veal into a basin, add gelatine mixture and mix well. Season to taste. Allow a little of the mixture to set in a small mould before adding the whole egg, and completely cover it with the remaining mixture. Allow to set. Remove carefully from mould and cut in half lengthwise. Serve both halves on a bed of watercress and garnish with chicory and radishes.

Place chicken and mushroom in a saucepan and cover with tomato juice. Add the Worcestershire sauce, garlic salt and curry powder. Bring to the boil and simmer for 15 minutes. Remove seeds from the green pepper and blanch in boiling, salted water for 3 – 5 minutes; drain, chop and add to curry with the chopped apple. Simmer for a further 5 minutes, serve on a bed of boiled cauliflower flowerets, accompanied by toast.

Stuffed Lambs Hearts

2 lambs hearts approximately 6 oz. each

$\frac{1}{2}$ pint water

1 teaspoon curry powder

1 teaspoon dried onion flakes

For stuffing:

2 oz. wholemeal breadcrumbs

1 tablespoon chopped parsley

1 celery stalk, chopped

Grated rind of 1 lemon

Pepper and salt

Chicken stock

Serves 2

Remove veins and fat from hearts then cut through centre divisions to make a cavity in each. Soak in salted water for 1 hour. Mix all ingredients for stuffing and bind with a little chicken stock. Use to stuff the drained hearts. Close with wooden cocktail sticks then place in small casserole. Pour over $\frac{1}{2}$ pt. water, the curry powder and onion flakes. Cover and cook in cool oven (300°F or Mark 2) for $2\frac{1}{2}$ hours or until tender, basting occasionally. Slice and serve with broccoli spears.

Chicken with Asparagus Sauce

1 lb. cooked diced chicken

1 8-oz. tin sliced green beans

1 8-oz. tin peppers, chopped

2 medium celery stalks, finely chopped

$\frac{1}{2}$ medium fresh green pepper, chopped

1 15-oz. tin asparagus, drained

$\frac{3}{4}$ pint skimmed milk

Serves 4

Mix together first 5 ingredients. Put asparagus and milk into blender and blend one minute at high speed. Transfer to saucepan and bring to boiling point. Add chicken/vegetable mixture and simmer about 5 minutes or until heated through.

Cheesy Chicken and Asparagus Salad

1 tin (approximately 12 oz.) asparagus tips

12 oz. chicken, cooked and diced

1 red eating apple, cooked and diced

Juice of $\frac{1}{2}$ lemon

4 oz. cottage cheese

Lettuce

Salt

Freshly ground black pepper

Mustard and cress

Decoration: parsley and strips of red pepper

Serves 4

Strain asparagus and put a few tips aside for garnish. Chop remainder and mix with chicken and cheese. Add the lemon juice to the diced red apple to prevent discolouration. Mix all ingredients thoroughly together. Season well and add a little mustard and cress. Serve on a bed of lettuce leaves and decorate with a few asparagus tips, strips of pepper and sprigs of parsley.

Chelsea Fare

4 chicken or rabbit leg joints

4 inches cucumber

4 oz. Cheshire cheese

1 tablespoon sage

$\frac{1}{2}$ pint stock

Seasoning

1 lb. mushrooms

4 bunches watercress

4 slices bread, crumbed

Serves 4

Bone the joints to leave 2 oz. meat in each case. Dice cucumber and half the cheese. Mix with sage. Put into cavities in meat. Secure joints with cocktail sticks. Rub with salt. Put into casserole. Pour over stock. Cover and bake in a moderate oven (350°F or Mark 4) for about $\frac{3}{4}$ hour. Add mushrooms for last half hour. Meanwhile, blanch watercress for about 3 minutes. Drain. Spread out on serving dish. Drain joints and mushrooms. Place on watercress. Sprinkle with remaining grated cheese and breadcrumbs. Brown under grill.

Egg and Cheese Salad

1 hard boiled egg

Dash of salt

Dash of onion powder

Dash of pepper

2 oz. cottage (or Cheshire) cheese

1 teaspoon finely chopped green pepper

Lettuce

Summer cabbage

2 tablespoons Weight Watchers mayonnaise

Serves 1

Chop egg and sprinkle with seasonings. Combine cheese with green pepper and toss lightly with egg. Serve on lettuce and bed of finely shredded cabbage. Serve with Weight Watchers mayonnaise.

Opposite: Chicken Curry

Stuffed Omelette with Melba Toast

2 oz. lean leftover meat from roast

4–6 mushrooms

¼ beef stock cube

Little tomato juice to moisten

¼ teaspoon dried onion flakes

Seasoning (garlic salt, ground black pepper and salt)

1 egg

1 slice bread, wholemeal if possible

Serves 1

Liquidize meat, mushrooms, stock cube, tomato juice, onion flakes and seasonings or, in absence of liquidizer, chop solids as finely as possible and mix well with liquids. Cook slowly over low flame in non-stick pan till heated through and mushrooms are soft. Make a one-egg omelette, place meat/mushroom mixture in centre, fold over and serve with melba toast. To make the toast, toast 1 oz. slice bread on both sides, slit through centre with sharp knife and toast soft side again.

Mushrooms baked with Cheese Stuffing

Cheese Sandwich Soufflé

1 slice bread

Little prepared mustard

1 oz. cheese

1 egg

¼ pint skimmed milk

Seasoning to taste

Serves 1

Make sandwich with bread, mustard and cheese. Place in small ovenproof dish. Beat egg with milk, season to taste, and pour over sandwich. Cover with foil and bake in moderate oven (350°F or Mark 4) for about 30 minutes. Serve while still hot with cauliflower or any No. 3 vegetables.

39

Eggs with Curried Vegetables

2 oz. red or green pepper, finely chopped

1 eating apple, thinly sliced

1 teaspoon dried onion flakes

Salt and pepper to taste

1 to 3 teaspoons curry powder (or to taste)

$\frac{1}{4}$ pint tomato juice or water

2 oz. mushrooms, peeled and chopped

2 hard boiled eggs, freshly boiled

Serves 1

Put first 6 ingredients into a pan and simmer, covered, for about 10 minutes or until pepper is tender. Add mushrooms and continue to simmer for a further 10 minutes. Slice hot eggs on to a plate or bed of cooked cauliflower and coat with curried vegetables. Serve straight away.

English Cheese Cakes

1 oz. white breadcrumbs

1 egg, beaten

1 oz. Cheddar cheese, grated

Salt and pepper to taste

1 dessertspoon dried onion flakes

Serves 1

Mix all ingredients well together to form a fairly thick paste. (If too thick, add a little skimmed milk.) Shape into round patties of approximately $\frac{1}{4}$-inch in thickness. Cook gently in non-stick frying pan for 5 minutes, turning frequently. Garnish with cucumber and/or mushrooms.

Stuffed Green Pepper

1 medium green pepper

$\frac{1}{2}$ slice bread

2 tablespoons skimmed milk

2 oz. Cheddar cheese, grated

2 tablespoons tomato juice

1 teaspoon dried onion flakes

Pinch mixed herbs

Salt

Pepper

Garlic powder (optional)

Serves 1

Egg and Mushroom Savoury

1 lb. spinach

2 hard boiled eggs

4 fresh mushrooms, chopped

$\frac{1}{2}$ teaspoon dry mustard

Dash of Worcestershire sauce

Salt and pepper

Serves 1

Slice eggs in half lengthwise and remove yolks. Put yolks into bowl and mash finely. Add all remaining ingredients and mix well. Return to egg white halves. Serve on blanched spinach leaves.

Cut top off pepper and put the cap to one side. Scoop out both core and seeds from pepper and wash carefully. Drop into boiling water and cook for about 3 minutes. Drain. Crumble bread and soften in the milk. Stir in other ingredients with a fork. Fill the pepper with this mixture, replace cap and stand in a baking dish with a little water. Cook at 350°F or Mark 4 for 30 to 35 minutes, or until tender, basting with water occasionally.

Courgette Omelette

1 egg
2 tablespoons skimmed milk
1 tablespoon chopped parsley
¼ teaspoon salt
¼ teaspoon pepper
4 oz. cooked courgettes, sliced
1 oz. Cheddar cheese, grated
Serves 1

Beat egg with milk, parsley and seasoning. Add courgettes. Transfer to preheated non-stick pan and cook over a moderate heat until centre is almost set (about 4 minutes). Top with cheese. Transfer to grill pan and grill until cheese melts.

Egg Boats

1 oz. breadcrumbs
1 oz. Cheddar cheese, grated
Good pinch of dry mustard
Dash of Worcestershire sauce
Salt and pepper
2 tablespoons skimmed milk
1 egg, separated
1 teaspoon tomato juice
Cayenne pepper
Small packet frozen spinach
Serves 1

Mix together first 6 ingredients and form into a flat cake. Place on a baking sheet or foil. Whisk egg white till stiff and spread over 'cake' making a hollow in the centre. Drop egg yolk into centre. Spoon tomato juice over yolk and sprinkle the whole with salt and cayenne pepper. Cook at 400°F or Mark 6 for 20 – 25 minutes until egg yolk is set and white is golden brown and crisp. Serve on a bed of the cooked spinach.

Cauliflower and Egg Puff

1 small cauliflower
2 slices bread
2 oz. Cheddar cheese, grated
2 eggs, separated
Salt and pepper to taste
Serves 2

Break cauliflower into flowerets and cook in boiling salted water for about 10 to 12 minutes. Meanwhile, toast bread and cut into small triangles. Drain cauliflower thoroughly and transfer to heat-proof dish. Cover with half the cheese. Beat egg whites until stiff. Spoon carefully over cauliflower, leaving two wells in the centre. Pour egg yolks into wells and season to taste with salt and pepper. Sprinkle remaining cheese over the top. Grill until the yolks are set and garnish with toast triangles.

Courgette and Mushroom Savoury

Courgettes as required
(3 – 4 per person according to size)
About 3 tablespoons chicken stock
4 oz. mushrooms
Lemon juice to taste
Pepper and salt
4 oz. Cheddar cheese, grated
2 slices bread, toasted
Serves 2

Place courgettes (topped and tailed) into boiling water and cook for 2 minutes to eliminate bitter taste. Drain and refresh under cold water. Cut into ¾ inch thick slices. Put into non-stick pan. Add stock and cook gently, with lid on pan, for about 15 minutes or until almost tender. Add sliced mushrooms, lemon juice and seasoning and cook, covered, a further 5 minutes. Uncover, increase heat and cook briskly for a moment or two to evaporate some of the liquid. Place mixture into two individual heatproof dishes, sprinkle 2 oz. cheese over each and brown under hot grill. Serve immediately accompanied by toast.

Apple Shell Salad

2 large eating apples

Lemon juice

4 radishes, sliced

2 teaspoons finely chopped green pepper

4 oz. prawns or shrimps

4 oz. cottage cheese

Seasoning to taste

Paprika

Lettuce leaves

Serves 2

Halve apples and remove cores. Scoop out flesh leaving $\frac{1}{4}$ inch-thick apple shells. Sprinkle with lemon juice. Chop flesh and mix with lemon juice and sliced radishes. Add this to the prawns, cottage cheese and green pepper and mix well together. Season lightly and pile into apple shells. Sprinkle with paprika. Serve two halves per person on lettuce leaves.

Mushrooms Baked with Cheese Stuffing

4 large fresh mushrooms

2 oz. Cheddar cheese

1 slice bread, toasted

2 tablespoons chopped parsley

Good pinch of onion powder

Good pinch of garlic powder

Salt

Freshly ground black pepper

Rind of $\frac{1}{4}$ lemon

1 teaspoon lemon juice

Watercress for garnish

Serves 1

Remove stems from mushrooms and place these in electric blender with cheese, bread, parsley and seasonings. Blend at high speed until smooth. Fill mushroom caps with the mixture. Bake in warm oven (325°F or Mark 3) for 15 to 20 minutes. Garnish with watercress before serving.

42

Prawn Omelette

2 oz. frozen prawns

1 egg

1 tablespoon skimmed milk

2 medium mushrooms, sliced

Seasoning to taste

Serves 1

De-frost prawns. Beat egg with milk. Add prawns and mushrooms. Season to taste with salt and pepper. Cook in non-stick omelette pan and accompany with a salad of No. 3 vegetables.

Opposite: Country Cabbage – unlimited

Eggs in Thick Curry Sauce

2 level teaspoons curry powder

$\frac{1}{4}$ pint water

Salt and pepper

Artificial liquid sweetener to equal 2 teaspoons sugar

8 oz. prepared marrow, boiled and well drained

$\frac{1}{4}$ lb. button mushrooms, sliced

1 large stick celery, chopped

2 hard boiled eggs

$\frac{1}{4}$ red pepper

$\frac{1}{4}$ green pepper

Serves 1

Dissolve curry powder in water in a pan with salt, pepper and sweetener and bring to the boil. Add the cooked marrow and mash well. Simmer for 5 minutes. Add mushrooms and celery, cover pan and simmer gently for 10 minutes. Cut eggs in half and cut peppers into thin strips. Add to the pan and simmer uncovered for 3 minutes or until eggs are heated through. Serve with boiled courgettes and garnish with chopped parsley.

Broccoli Cheese

9 oz. packet frozen broccoli or
½ lb. fresh broccoli

Salt and pepper

2 oz. Cheddar cheese, grated

1 oz. white breadcrumbs

Serves 1

Cook the broccoli in boiling water until tender. Drain and reserve 2 tablespoons of the cooking liquid. Place broccoli in a shallow ovenproof dish, pour over liquid and season with salt and pepper. Mix cheese and breadcrumbs and sprinkle over broccoli. Put under a moderate grill until cheese has melted and is golden brown.

Cottage Cheese Medley

4 oz. cottage cheese

Lettuce or finely chopped white cabbage

1 orange cut into segments

Low calorie orange squash, if desired

1 slice bread, toasted, cut into fingers

Serves 1

Arrange cottage cheese on bed of lettuce leaves or white cabbage. Decorate with orange segments. If a more pronounced orange flavour is desired, pour a little low-calorie orange squash over cottage cheese before decorating with orange. Serve on toast fingers.

Peach and Cottage Cheese Salad

Crisp leaves of lettuce

⅓ cucumber

Lemon juice

1 fresh peach

4 oz. cottage cheese

Strips of tinned peppers

1 slice bread, toasted

Serves 1

Line plate with lettuce. Grate cucumber and arrange on top of lettuce. Sprinkle with lemon juice. Peel, halve and stone peach and stand on plate, sprinkle with a little more lemon juice and then fill cavities with cottage cheese. Decorate with strips of pepper and accompany with toast.

Devilled Buck

1 slice toast

1 oz. Cheddar cheese, thinly sliced

½ dessert apple, thinly sliced

Curry powder

1 egg

Sliced green beans, cooked

Serves 1

Cover toast completely with slices of cheese, then top with apple slices. Sprinkle with curry powder to taste. Place under low to medium grill until apple is tender and cheese is beginning to melt. Top with a poached egg and serve with green beans.

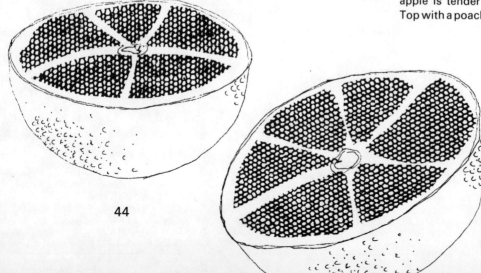

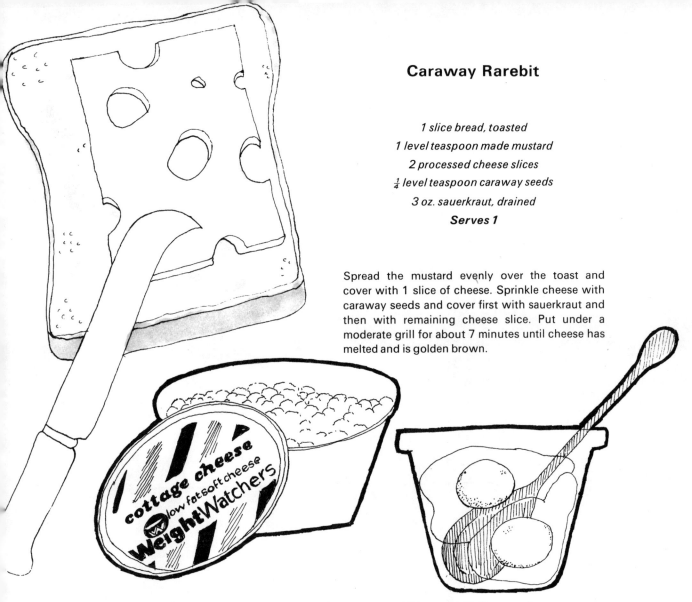

Caraway Rarebit

1 slice bread, toasted
1 level teaspoon made mustard
2 processed cheese slices
¼ level teaspoon caraway seeds
3 oz. sauerkraut, drained
Serves 1

Spread the mustard evenly over the toast and cover with 1 slice of cheese. Sprinkle cheese with caraway seeds and cover first with sauerkraut and then with remaining cheese slice. Put under a moderate grill for about 7 minutes until cheese has melted and is golden brown.

Party Cheese

3 tablespoons water
3 tablespoons cider vinegar
Artificial sweetener to equal 1 teaspoon sugar or to taste
4 oz. Cheddar cheese cut into small cubes
8 oz. cottage cheese
4 slices bread, toasted, cut into fingers
Serves 4

Combine all ingredients, except bread, in blender. Run at low speed for 1 minute or until mixture is smooth and well-mixed. Chill well in refrigerator. Divide between four plates. Serve on lettuce leaves with crisp fingers of celery, slices of cucumber and fingers of toast.

"Potato" Pancakes

1 small cauliflower
1 slice bread
2 eggs, well beaten
Dash of salt
¼ teaspoon dried onion flakes
1 tablespoon skimmed milk
Serves 1

Cook cauliflower in salted water until quite soft. Drain thoroughly. Mash with a fork until very smooth. Place bread in blender to make breadcrumbs. Combine mashed cauliflower and breadcrumbs with all remaining ingredients. Drop tablespoons of mixture into heated non-stick pan. When brown, turn over and brown other side.

Cucumber and Radishes with Weight Watchers Sauce – unlimited

Above: Cauliflower and Pepper Salad – unlimited   Below: Green Bean Salad – unlimited

Golden Coated Cauliflower

1 small cauliflower
1 tablespoon skimmed milk
½ teaspoon made mustard
Salt and pepper
2 oz. Cheddar cheese, grated
1 oz. white breadcrumbs
Serves 1

Cook the cauliflower in boiling salted water until tender. Drain thoroughly and place in a shallow dish. Put milk, mustard, seasoning and cheese into a small pan and heat gently until melted. Spoon over the cauliflower, sprinkle with breadcrumbs and put under a medium grill until top is golden brown. Serve with a green salad.

Braised Fennel – unlimited

2 – 3 bulbs of fennel
1 beef cube
½ pint water
Serves 2

Wash and remove bruised outer skins. Cut into quarters and simmer for 20 minutes in stock.

Mushrooms in thick Beef Gravy – unlimited

½ pint water
1 lb. marrow, peeled, seeded and diced
2 beef cubes
2 tablespoons dried onion flakes
¼ lb. sliced fresh mushrooms
Serves 2

Combine water, marrow and beef cubes together and cook until marrow is tender. Remove from heat and puree in blender. Return to saucepan. Add sliced mushrooms and simmer for 10 minutes, stirring constantly until mushrooms are cooked.

48

Country Cabbage – unlimited

1 medium head of cabbage
1 tablespoon salt
¼ pint water approx.
4 celery stalks, diced
1 red pepper, diced
1 bunch watercress, chopped
For dressing:
6 tablespoons water
¼ pint distilled malt vinegar
2 teaspoons artificial sweetener
1 teaspoon celery seeds
Serves 4

Shred cabbage finely. Place in bowl, sprinkle the layers with salt and water. Leave for two hours, then pick it up by the handful and squeeze out the juice. Place the cabbage in another bowl and add celery, red pepper and watercress. Combine all dressing ingredients. Stir well, pour over vegetables and toss well.

Chicory in Bouillon – unlimited

1 lb. chicory
¾ pint water
1 chicken stock cube
2 tablespoons chopped parsley
Serves 2

Remove any discoloured outside leaves from chicory and discard. Bring water to the boil in a saucepan, add stock cube and stir until dissolved. Add whole chicory and cook for about 10 minutes or until outer leaves are soft. Serve sprinkled with parsley.

Green Peppers in Piquant Sauce — unlimited

2 to 3 medium green peppers
For sauce:
$\frac{1}{4}$ pint tomato juice
1 tablespoon Worcestershire sauce
1 tablespoon horse-radish
1 tablespoon cider vinegar
Artificial sweetener to taste
Serves 2

Make the sauce first. Mix all ingredients well together and leave for 1 hour. Wash peppers and place whole under a hot grill, turning continuously until all the skin has been scorched. Hold under cold tap and remove skin. Cut peppers into two, remove stalk, seeds and pith and cut flesh into long strips. Put into a dish and coat with sauce. Serve chilled.

Weight Watchers Ratatouille — unlimited

$\frac{1}{2}$ pint tomato juice
1 chicken stock cube
2 level teaspoons dried onion flakes
2 level teaspoons dried pepper flakes
2 tablespoons wine vinegar
Artificial liquid sweetener to equal
4 teaspoons sugar
Salt and pepper
1 small marrow
Serves 4

Put tomato juice, stock cube, onion and pepper flakes, vinegar, sweetener and seasoning in a pan and bring to the boil. Simmer gently until pepper has reconstituted — about 5 minutes. Peel, core and dice marrow and add to the pan. Cover and simmer gently for about 20 minutes until marrow is tender.

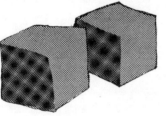

Mustard Cabbage — unlimited

4 tablespoons dried onion flakes
1 small cabbage
1 green pepper
1 small tin red peppers, drained
2 teaspoons salt
For dressing:
$\frac{1}{4}$ pint plus 4 tablespoons cider vinegar
Artificial sweetener to equal 4 teaspoons sugar,
or to taste
$\frac{1}{4}$ pint plus 4 tablespoons water
1 tablespoon mustard seeds
Serves 2

Soak onion flakes in hot water to soften. Shred cabbage. Chop peppers. Combine all ingredients with salt and cover with dressing.
To make dressing, combine all indicated ingredients. Bring to boil and pour over vegetables.

Courgettes in Tomato Juice — unlimited

1 lb. courgettes
$\frac{1}{2}$ pint tomato juice
$\frac{1}{4}$ pint water
2 tablespoons cider vinegar
1 chicken stock cube
2 teaspoons dried pepper flakes
2 teaspoons dried onion flakes
2 teaspoons dried celery flakes
Serves 2

Top and tail courgettes and cut into fingers. Transfer to a bowl of cold water. Place all other ingredients in a saucepan and bring to boil. Simmer for 10 minutes, add courgettes and cover pan. Cook gently until courgettes are tender, adding a little extra water if liquid reduces too much.

Crunchy Soy Cabbage – unlimited

½ small white cabbage

4 fl. oz. tomato juice

2 tablespoons soy sauce

Salt and pepper

Serves 1 – 2

Shred the cabbage finely. Place other ingredients in a saucepan and mix thoroughly. Add cabbage and coat in the liquid. Bring to the boil, cover pan and simmer gently for about 15 minutes until cabbage is tender but still slightly crunchy.

Green Dragon Salad – unlimited

1 Cos lettuce

½ large cucumber

White heart of cabbage

1 bunch watercress

For dressing:

2 tablespoons wine or cider vinegar

½ teaspoon made mustard

Salt and pepper to taste

Artificial sweetener to taste

Serves 4

Shred all vegetables finely and put into large bowl. Beat dressing ingredients well together. Pour over salad and toss well.

Green Melody – unlimited

½ cucumber, sliced

6 oz. white heart of cabbage, finely shredded

½ Cos or 1 small Cos lettuce, shredded

2 tablespoons wine vinegar

½ level teaspoon made mustard

Salt and pepper

Artificial sweetener to equal
1 teaspoon sugar

Watercress

Serves 4

Mix together cucumber, cabbage and lettuce in a bowl. Combine vinegar, mustard, salt, pepper and sweetener and pour over salad. Toss. Decorate salad with sprig of watercress.

Sunset Chou

2 lb. red cabbage

¼ pint chicken stock

3 red apples, cored and sliced

2 tablespoons dried onion flakes

1 clove garlic, finely chopped

2 – 4 tablespoons wine vinegar

Artificial sweetener to equal
2 tablespoons sugar

3 whole cloves

Salt, freshly ground black pepper to taste

Grated nutmeg to taste

Serves 4

Wash and shred cabbage. Place in saucepan with remaining ingredients. Cover and simmer until tender but still crisp – about 30 minutes.

Spinach Salad – unlimited

1 lb. seakale beet spinach

1 tablespoon lemon juice

3 tablespoons chicken stock, made from bouillon cube

$\frac{1}{4}$ teaspoon salt

$\frac{1}{4}$ teaspoon Worcestershire sauce

Artificial sweetener to equal 1 teaspoon sugar

Serves 4

Remove stalks from seakale beet spinach, chop and place in a large saucepan. Wash leaves well; drain. Place on top of chopped stalks, add no water, cover. Steam 3 minutes, or just until leaves wilt; drain any liquid from pan. In a basin, combine lemon juice, stock, salt, Worcestershire sauce and sweetener. Pour over spinach. Toss to coat leaves well. Serve hot or chilled.

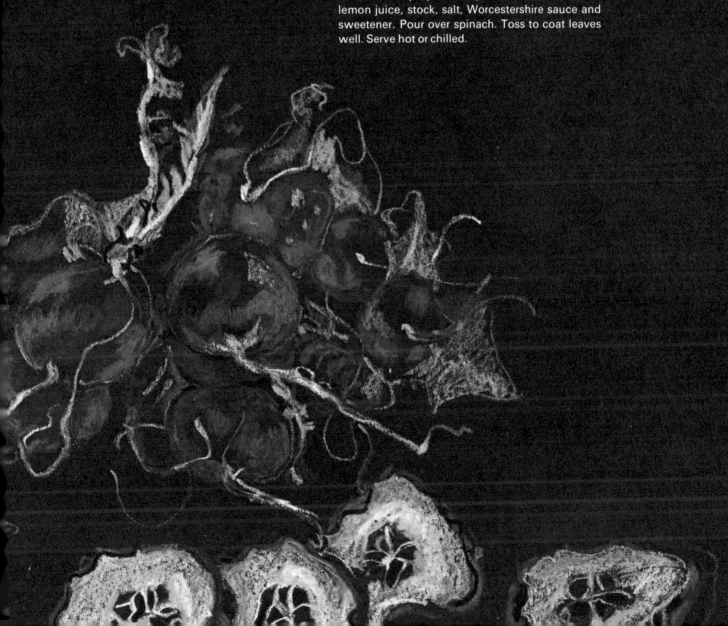

Windsor Slaw and Dressing

1 white cabbage
1 eating apple
1 teaspoon dried onion flakes
Cucumber, sliced
Radishes, large, sliced
For Salad Dressing:
2 tablespoons lemon juice
3 tablespoons water
$\frac{1}{2}$ teaspoon salt
$\frac{1}{4}$ teaspoon dry mustard
$\frac{1}{4}$ teaspoon pepper
Serves 4

Shred cabbage finely, peel apple and grate coarsely and mix both together with onion flakes. Then sprinkle with lemon juice and place mixture in bowl lined with cucumber slices; garnish with radish slices. Serve with salad dressing.

Cauliflower and Pepper Salad – unlimited

1 small to medium cauliflower
1 red and 1 green pepper
2 celery stalks
2 oz. mushrooms (raw)
2 tablespoons lemon juice
4 tablespoons tomato juice
2 teaspoons Worcestershire sauce
1 teaspoon salt
1 teaspoon horse-radish
Artificial sweetener to taste
Few sprigs parsley for garnish
Serves 2

Coarsely chop cauliflower, de-seed pepper and cut into dice. Slice celery stalks diagonally and raw mushrooms thinly. Put all vegetables into a salad bowl. Beat all remaining ingredients well together. Pour over salad and toss well. Garnish with parsley.

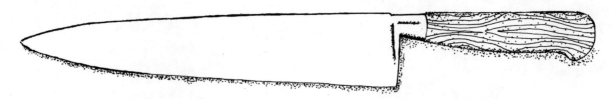

Cabbage and Pepper Salad – unlimited

1 small head of white cabbage
1 medium red or green pepper
$\frac{1}{2}$ teaspoon caraway seeds
1 teaspoon prepared mustard
1 heaped tablespoon chopped parsley
2 teaspoons soy sauce
Salt, pepper and artificial sweetener to taste
Serves 2

Shred cabbage finely. Cut pepper into thin strips. Put both into salad bowl. Beat all remaining ingredients well together. Pour on to salad and toss.

Green Bean Salad – unlimited

1 medium tin or frozen pack runner beans
3 – 4 stalks celery, diced
$\frac{1}{2}$ teaspoon dried onion flakes
1 small tin of peppers, drained and chopped
2 large gherkins, chopped
1 medium cucumber, sliced
3 tablespoons tarragon vinegar
3 tablespoons white wine vinegar
Artificial sugar sweetener to taste
Freshly ground black pepper
Serves 2 – 3 – unlimited

Mix all ingredients in a large bowl, season well. Cover and let stand in a refrigerator overnight.

Apple Queen Pudding

5 tablespoons skimmed milk

Artificial sweetener to taste

1 slice bread, white, crumbed

1 egg

1 medium eating apple

Serves 1

Warm milk with 3 sweetener tablets. Pour over the crumbed bread and leave for 10 minutes. Separate egg and add yolk to bread mixture. Bake in a moderate oven (350°F or Mark 4) for 15 to 20 minutes. Slice apple and stew with 4 table-spoons water and sweetener tablets. Pour over top of bread mixture and cover with stiffly beaten egg white (with 3 crushed sweetener tablets added) and bake for approximately 8 minutes in a fairly hot oven (400°F or Mark 6).

Apple Meringue

4 oz. cooking apples

1 egg, separated

1 oz. breadcrumbs

$\frac{1}{2}$ teaspoon cinnamon

Rind of $\frac{1}{4}$ lemon

Artificial sweetener to taste

Serves 1

Peel and core apples and place in a saucepan with 1 tablespoon of water. Cook until tender. While apples are still hot stir in egg yolk, breadcrumbs, cinnamon, lemon rind and sweetener to taste. Transfer to ovenproof dish. Beat egg white until stiff and then add 1 – 2 teaspoons of liquid sweetener. Spoon over apple mixture. Cook in a cool oven at 300°F or Mark 2 for about 20 – 30 minutes or until puffed up and pale golden.

Apple Crumble

1 oz. white breadcrumbs

Grated peel of 1 lemon

1 medium-sized cooking apple,
peeled and sliced

1 tablespoon lemon juice

Little artificial sweetener if necessary

3 slices of lemon, to decorate

Serves 1

Mix breadcrumbs and lemon rind together. Slowly cook apple in lemon juice in a covered pan until soft. Add a little artificial sweetener if necessary. Line a small individual pie dish with half of the breadcrumbs. Spoon in apple and cover with remaining breadcrumbs. Bake in a fairly hot oven (375°F or Mark 5) for approximately 40 minutes, or until golden brown and crisp. Decorate with lemon slices.

Mock Apple Pastry

1 slice white bread

1 apple, peeled, cored and sliced

1 teaspoon lemon juice

1 tablespoon water

$\frac{1}{4}$ level teaspoon cinnamon

Artificial sweetener to equal
1 tablespoon sugar

Serves 1

Cook last 5 ingredients with the apple in a covered pan until tender. Cool. Remove crust from bread and roll with a rolling pin to make slice thinner. Place apple mixture on half of bread, fold diagonally, moisten edges, press together with fork. Bake in a hot oven (425°F or Mark 7) approximately 15 to 20 minutes, until brown. The same recipe can be baked at 350°F or Mark 4 until crisp.

**Apple Queen
Pudding**

Apple Crumble

Apple Meringue

Rhubarb Fool

Rhubarb Jelly

1 lb. rhubarb, prepared
¼ pint low-calorie lemon squash
Piece of lemon rind
6 – 8 saccharin tablets
½ oz. powdered gelatine
Serves 4

Cut rhubarb into 1½-inch lengths and stew in the lemon squash with lemon rind. Sweeten to taste with saccharin and cool slightly. Dissolve gelatine with 2 tablespoons water in a basin over a pan of hot water and stir into rhubarb mixture. Pour into a serving bowl and leave to set in a cool place. Serve with cream made from ½ oz. skimmed milk powder and 1 tablespoon water mixed together.

Rhubarb Russe

½ lb. rhubarb, prepared
5 tablespoons blackcurrant or orange low-calorie squash
Artificial liquid sweetener to equal 4 teaspoons sugar
1 oz. white breadcrumbs
Serves 1

Stew the rhubarb gently with 4 tablespoons of squash in a covered pan. Add sweetener and beat till smooth. Put rhubarb in an individual ovenproof dish and spoon remaining squash over the fruit. Cover with breadcrumbs and cook at 400°F or Mark 6 for about 30 – 40 minutes until breadcrumbs are crispy and golden brown.

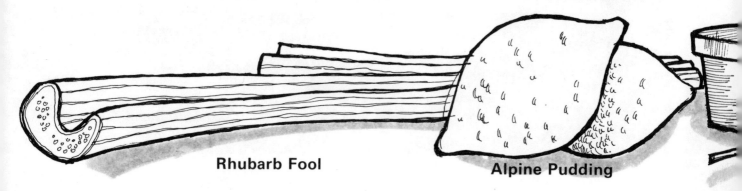

Rhubarb Fool

1 lb. fresh rhubarb cut into 2-inch lengths
2 tablespoons water
10 drops artificial liquid sweetener
2 eggs
¼ pint plus 3 dessertspoons skimmed milk, warmed
8 drops artificial liquid sweetener
2 slices lemon, to decorate
Serves 2

Stew rhubarb in water with 10 drops of sweetener till tender. Cool and then put through a sieve or liquidize and blend until smooth. Beat eggs together and combine with the warmed milk and sweetener. Strain into a pan and cook gently until thick, stirring all the time. Mix custard with rhubarb and add more sweetener if necessary. Chill in refrigerator. Pour into glasses. To serve, decorate with slices of lemon.

Alpine Pudding

1 oz. white breadcrumbs
4 oz. skimmed milk
1 egg, separated
Grated rind of ½ lemon
Little stewed rhubarb
Artificial liquid sweetener
Serves 1

Place the crumbs in an ovenproof dish. Mix together thoroughly the milk, egg yolk, liquid sweetener to equal 3 teaspoons sugar and lemon rind. Pour over breadcrumbs and allow to soak completely. Cook at 325°F or Mark 3 for about 20 minutes until set. Cover with a thin layer of stewed rhubarb. Whisk egg white till stiff. Stir in liquid sweetener to equal 1 teaspoon sugar and spread over the rhubarb. Return to the oven for 10 – 15 minutes until meringue is pale golden.

Apricot Pancakes

1 large egg
1 slice bread, without crust
Artificial sweetener to equal 2 teaspoons sugar
2 oz. cottage cheese
2 fresh apricots, stoned and diced
Sprigs of watercress to garnish
Serves 1

Combine egg, bread and sweetener. Liquidize at medium speed for 1 minute or until mixture is consistency of batter. Cook as pancakes in hot non-stick pan until cooked throughout. Turn once. Fill with diced apricot and cottage cheese. Decorate with sprigs of watercress and serve.

Sunshine Orange Soufflé

7 fl. oz. skimmed milk
2 artificial sweetener tablets
2 medium-sized oranges
2 slices bread, without crust
2 eggs, separated
Serves 2

Grate orange skins finely. Cut 1 slice from the middle of each orange – squeeze juice from ends, mix with grated rind and stir well. Heat milk with sweetener, but do not boil. Cut bread into small cubes and add to milk. Add orange juice and rind and continue stirring. Take off heat and add two beaten egg yolks. Quickly fold in stiffly beaten egg whites. Pour into a casserole dish. Place orange slices on top. Cook in a fairly hot oven (375°F or Mark 5) for 5 minutes, then increase to 400°F or Mark 6 for a further 20 to 25 minutes, or until golden brown and puffed.

Vanilla Peach Dream

1 slice white bread
1 fresh peach, peeled and sliced
$\frac{1}{8}$ level teaspoon cinnamon
$\frac{1}{4}$ pint plus 2 tablespoons skimmed milk, scalded
$\frac{1}{4}$ teaspoon vanilla essence
Artificial sweetener to equal 6 teaspoons sugar
Serves 1

Break bread into small pieces and arrange in a shallow ovenproof dish. Arrange peach slices over bread and sprinkle with the cinnamon. Liquidize milk, egg, vanilla and sweetener. Blend at high speed for 30 seconds. Pour milk mixture over peach and bread. Lift a few pieces of bread to help make a crust. Bake in a warm oven (325°F or Mark 3) for about 40 minutes or until set.

Orange Angel Dessert

2 eggs
$\frac{1}{2}$ pint skimmed milk, warmed
4 artificial sweetener tablets
1 orange
Serves 2

Divide eggs. Beat yolk of eggs with milk. Add sweetener and grated rind of orange. Bake in a moderate oven (350°F or Mark 4) until almost set, about 30 minutes. Beat whites of eggs stiffly and spoon on top of the custard. Return to oven and brown. Serve with sliced orange.

Orange Pudding

½ pint skimmed milk

1 orange

1 egg, separated

Liquid artificial sweetener to equal
3 teaspoons sugar

1 slice of bread

Nutmeg

Serves 1

Heat milk and the peel of the orange slowly for 10 minutes. **Do not boil.** Strain and cool slightly. Whisk milk with the egg yolk and add sweetener to taste. Whisk egg white until stiff and fold into milk mixture. Put the bread in the base of an ovenproof dish and pour custard on top. Sprinkle with nutmeg. Place dish in a shallow pan of water and bake in a moderate oven (350°F or Mark 4) for 50 – 60 minutes until set and golden brown. Serve hot or cold garnished with orange segments.

Opposite, left:
Apricot Pancakes

Opposite, right:
Sunshine Orange Soufflé

Opposite, below left:
Orange Angel Dessert

Opposite, below right:
Ice Cold Peppermint Grapefruit
and Cinnamon Fingers

Windsor Bread Pudding

¼ pint plus 4 tablespoons skimmed milk

1 egg

Artificial sweetener to equal 2 tablespoons sugar

¼ teaspoon vanilla essence

1 slice white bread

Serves 1

Scald milk. Mix together egg, artificial sweetener and vanilla essence. Add egg mixture to milk. Break bread into small chunks in baking dish. Pour egg and milk mixture over bread, allowing a few pieces to float on top. Bake in a warm oven (325°F or Mark 3) for about 20 to 25 minutes. Serve hot or cold.

Cheesecake Fiesta

4 egg yolks

½ pint skimmed milk

Artificial sweetener to equal 4 teaspoons sugar

1 oz. powdered gelatine

12 oz. cottage cheese

3 tablespoons lemon juice

1 teaspoon grated lemon peel

1 teaspoon vanilla essence

½ level teaspoon salt

Artificial sweetener to equal 2 teaspoons sugar

4 egg whites

Serves 8

Cook first 4 ingredients over simmering water stirring constantly until mixture thickens sufficiently to coat back of spoon. Add cottage cheese. Then either rub mixture through a sieve or put into liqui-dizer and run until smooth. Add lemon juice, peel and vanilla essence. Set aside until cold but not set. Beat last 3 ingredients together until stiff, then fold into cheese mixture. Pour into a mould and chill until firm.

Ice Cold Peppermint Grapefruit and Cinnamon Fingers

1 grapefruit

3 – 4 drops peppermint essence

3 – 4 drops green colouring

Artificial liquid sweetener to taste

2 slices bread

Cinnamon

Twist of lemon peel to decorate

Serves 2

Peel grapefruit down to flesh with a sharp knife and cut away segments between the membranes. Put juice to one side. Place segments in two glasses. Measure 4 tablespoons grapefruit juice and add peppermint essence, green colouring and liquid sweetener (to equal 2 teaspoons sugar or more if liked). Spoon liquid over grapefruit segments and chill thoroughly. Serve with bread fingers which have been dusted lightly with cinnamon and toasted.

DINNER

Soups and Hors d'Oeuvres

Cream of Celery Soup/**62**
Thick Creamed Cauliflower Soup/**62**
Cream of Onion Soup/**62**
Cabbage and Celery Soup – unlimited/**62**
Illimité Soup – unlimited/**63**
Jellied Grapefruit Consommé/**63**
Melon Cooler/**64**
Red Cabbage with Apple/**64**
Cucumber and Radishes with Creole Sauce/**64**
Spicy Baked Tomatoes/**64**
Salad Crunch/**65**
Sweet Sour Cauliflower – unlimited/**65**
Salad Appetizer – unlimited/**65**
Carrot Hors d'Oeuvre/**65**
Savoury Orange Jelly/**66**

Main Dishes

Poached Mussels/**68**
King-Crab Special/**68**
Grilled Salmon/**68**
Mackerel in Foil/**68**
Mackerel Rosemary/**69**
Quickie Fish Cakes/**69**
Cod Exotic/**69**
Cod Steak Toledo/**69**
Cod Kebabs/**71**
Fish Piquant/**71**
Poached Haddock with Salmon/**72**
Baked Haddock in Sauce/**72**
Whiting with French Mustard Sauce/**72**
Norwegian Fish Salad/**73**
Baked Garlic White Fish/**73**
Halibut Special/**73**
Baked Lemon Sole/**73**
Mushroom Stuffed Fish/**75**
Weight Watchers Dry Fry/**75**
Madras Beef Curry/**76**
Spring Thyme Mince/**76**
Sweet and Sour Liver/**76**
Weight Watchers "Shepherds Pie"/**76**
Liver and Apple Casserole/**77**
Liver Baked in Foil/**77**
Liver Kababs/**77**
Liver Italienne/**77**

Veal Roll/**78**
Roast Pheasant (with Festive Fruit Sauce)/**78**
Frankfurters in Tomato Sauce/**78**
Chicken Special/**80**
Tomato Chicken Bake/**80**
Sweet Sour Chicken/**80**
Jellied Chicken/**81**
Austrian Peppers/**81**
Braised Chicken in Foil/**81**

Vegetables and Salads

Baked Aubergines/**81**
Braised Leeks/**82**
Curried Parsnips/**82**
Sprouts with Celery/**82**
Baked Marrow Savoury/**82**
Spiced Beetroot/**82**
Artichokes in Tomato Jelly/**84**
Artichokes Citrus/**84**
Tomato Platter/**84**
Orange and Chicory Salad/**84**
Peking Salad/**85**
Spiced Vegetable Stew/**85**
Evening Salad/**85**

Desserts

Orange Strawberry Whip/**88**
Strawberry Soufflé/**88**
Strawberry "Cream"/**88**
Tutti Frutti Mix/**89**
Stewed Rhubarb – unlimited/**89**
Fruit Fool/**89**
Raspberry Tang/**89**
Mandarin Soufflé/**92**
Orange Cocktail/**92**
Lemon Ice – unlimited/**92**
Vanilla Junket/**92**
Coffee Vanilla Cream/**93**
Melon Mould/**93**
Mock Melon Surprise – unlimited/**93**

Cream of Celery Soup

1 head celery

2 beef or chicken cubes

$\frac{3}{4}$ pint hot water

1 — 2 tablespoons skimmed milk powder

Serves 2

Wash celery and coarsely chop. Dissolve stock cubes in hot water. Add celery and cook until tender. Liquidize or beat until smooth. Return to pan, stir in milk and reheat without boiling.

Thick Creamed Cauliflower Soup

1 medium-sized cauliflower

2 beef or chicken stock cubes

$\frac{3}{4}$ pint hot water

1 — 2 tablespoons skimmed milk powder

Serves 2

Wash and break cauliflower into flowerets. Dissolve stock cubes in hot water. Add cauliflower and cook until tender. Liquidize or beat until smooth with egg whisk. Return to pan and stir in skimmed milk. Reheat without boiling.

Cream of Onion Soup

$\frac{1}{4}$ pint skimmed milk

1 tablespoon dried onion flakes

1 chicken stock cube

Serves 1

Combine all ingredients in saucepan. Cook over low heat, stirring frequently, for 10 minutes.

Cabbage and Celery Soup – unlimited

$1\frac{1}{2}$ lb. white cabbage (Dutch type)

4 medium-sized celery stalks

1 pint tomato juice

1 tablespoon dried onion flakes

1 teaspoon Worcestershire sauce

Salt and pepper to taste

$1\frac{1}{2}$ pints water

Serves 4

Shred cabbage finely. Chop celery. Put both into large saucepan with all remaining ingredients. Bring to boil and lower heat. Cover and simmer for about 30 minutes or until vegetables are soft. To make cream style soup, put into blender and blend until completely smooth. Reheat before serving.

Jellied Grapefruit Consommé

Illimité Soup — unlimited

½ pint plus 4 tablespoons tomato juice
¾ pint beef stock
8 oz. cabbage, shredded
1 celery stalk, sliced
4 tablespoons dried onion flakes
1 tablespoon dried parsley flakes
1 teaspoon dried pepper flakes
Artificial sweetener to equal 1 teaspoon sugar
Dash garlic salt
Salt and pepper to taste
1 tin (4 oz.) sliced mushrooms, with liquid
1 tin (16 oz.) sliced green beans, with liquid
Serves 4 — 6

Combine all ingredients except mushrooms and beans. Cook until vegetables are tender. Add mushrooms, beans and liquid from both. Heat and serve.

Jellied Grapefruit Consommé

Juice of 1 grapefruit
Cold water
1 envelope of gelatine
Artificial sweetener to taste
¼ cucumber, chopped
Salt
Freshly ground black pepper
Chopped mint
Serves 2

Make up grapefruit juice to ¾ pint with cold water. Pour into saucepan and add gelatine. Stir over a low heat until gelatine dissolves. Sweeten to taste, then chill until the mixture begins to thicken. Stir in the chopped cucumber, season to taste. Leave in a cool place to set until firm. Chop and pile in two glasses. Garnish with chopped mint leaves sprinkled over the top.

Melon Cooler

1 wedge of honeydew melon
Lemon juice
Powdered ginger
Serves 1

Sprinkle melon liberally with lemon juice, then dust with ginger. Serve as cold as possible.

Red Cabbage with Apple

8 oz. pickled red cabbage
1 apple
1 teaspoon dried onion flakes
Serves 1

Put cabbage into bowl. Peel apple and grate. Add apple and onion flakes to cabbage and toss. Serve as cold as possible.

Spicy Baked Tomatoes

1 lb. tomatoes, about 8 medium-sized, halved
1 tablespoon prepared mustard
1 tablespoon dried onion flakes
2 tablespoons green pepper, chopped
2 tablespoons celery, chopped
½ teaspoon salt
4 tablespoons skimmed milk
Serves 4

Put tomatoes, cut side up, in a baking dish. Spread tops with mustard. Combine onion flakes, green pepper, celery and salt. Sprinkle over tomatoes. Spoon milk equally over each tomato half. Bake at 400°F or Mark 6 for about 15 minutes.

Cucumber and Radishes with Creole Sauce

½ cucumber
1 bunch radishes
For sauce:
½ pint tomato juice
2 tablespoons chopped green pepper
½ teaspoon salt
2 tablespoons wine vinegar
1 teaspoon Worcestershire sauce
½ teaspoon dry mustard
Serves 4

Combine all sauce ingredients in liquidizer, blend well and serve with fingers of cucumbers and radishes.

Salad Crunch

4 oz. shredded cabbage

4 oz. cooked peas

2 celery stalks

1 small red or green pepper

2 tablespoons lemon juice

1 tablespoon cider vinegar

Liquid artificial sweetener to equal
1 dessertspoon sugar

1 level teaspoon made mustard

1 level teaspoon salt

1 heaped tablespoon chopped parsley

Serves 1

Put cabbage and peas into bowl. Cut celery into diagonal slices, and cut seeded pepper into strips. Add to bowl. Beat all remaining ingredients well together and pour over salad ingredients. Toss well.

Salad Appetizer — unlimited

1 tin sauerkraut

2 oz. green pepper, diced

4 oz. celery, diced

1 tablespoon dried onion flakes

2 tablespoons liquid sweetener

1 teaspoon Worcestershire sauce

$\frac{1}{2}$ teaspoon dry mustard

2 tablespoons wine vinegar

Salt and pepper, to taste

Garlic salt, if liked

Serves 4

Drain sauerkraut well and mix with other ingredients. Chill thoroughly before serving.

Carrot Hors d'Oeuvre

Sweet Sour Cauliflower — unlimited

1 medium-sized cooked cauliflower

For sauce:

3 tablespoons lemon juice

1 tablespoon cider vinegar

Liquid artificial sweetener to equal 2 oz. sugar

$\frac{1}{2}$ teaspoon garlic salt

1 teaspoon Worcestershire sauce

$\frac{1}{2}$ teaspoon paprika

$\frac{1}{2}$ teaspoon salt

Serves 2 – 3

4 oz. carrots, peeled and grated

4 oz. mushrooms, thinly sliced

1 red-skinned apple, chopped

For sauce:

1 tablespoon lemon juice

1 teaspoon mixed herbs

$\frac{1}{2}$ teaspoon paprika

$\frac{1}{2}$ onion salt

1 teaspoon Worcestershire sauce

Ground black pepper

Artificial sweetener to taste

Serves 1

Break cauliflower into flowerets and put into dish. Beat all remaining ingredients well together. Pour over cauliflower. Cover and refrigerate for at least 2 hours.

Toss apple in lemon juice to prevent discoloration. Then put apple, carrots and mushrooms in a dish in neat rows. Beat all sauce ingredients well together. Pour over vegetables and chill.

**Opposite:
Carrot Hors d'Oe**

**Spicy Baked
Tomatoes**

Savoury Orange Jelly

1 envelope gelatine
½ pint plus 4 tablespoons water
½ chicken stock cube
1 teaspoon onion salt
¼ teaspoon salt
4 fl. oz. fresh orange juice
1 tablespoon lemon juice
4 oz. grated raw carrot

Serves 4

Soften gelatine in 4 tablespoons of cold water. Add salt and onion salt, ½ stock cube and rest of water. Stir over low heat until dissolved. Add orange and lemon juice and set aside to stiffen slightly. Add raw carrot to gelatine mixture and pour into 1 pint mould that has been rinsed in cold water. Chill. Unmould on lettuce leaves.

Poached Mussels

½ pint plus 4 tablespoons chicken stock
2 teaspoons dried marjoram
¼ teaspoon dried basil
1 tablespoon garlic salt
⅛ teaspoon peppercorns
1½ lb. cooked fresh mussels
Serves 4

Combine chicken stock, marjoram, basil, garlic salt and peppercorns. Pour over mussels in bowl. Let stand 2 hours. Transfer to pot. Cook over moderate heat for 5 minutes or until heated through.

Grilled Salmon

4 fresh salmon steaks, each 10 oz.
2 tablespoons chicken stock
Paprika
2 tablespoons cider vinegar
4 lemon wedges
Watercress
Serves 4

Place salmon steaks in a grill pan and pour over 1 tablespoon stock. Sprinkle with paprika and 1 tablespoon cider vinegar. Grill about 3 inches from source of heat for 5 minutes. Turn salmon. Pour remaining stock over fish, then sprinkle with paprika and rest of cider vinegar. Grill 5 minutes longer or until fish flakes easily with a fork. Garnish each steak with a wedge of lemon and watercress.

King-Crab Special

2 celery stalks
¼ pint plus 4 tablespoons chicken stock
2 tablespoons lemon juice
1 teaspoon almond essence (or less to taste)
12 oz. King-crab
Serves 2

Cut celery crosswise into ¼-inch pieces. Combine with next three ingredients. Leave to stand for 1 hour. Add King-crab. Cook over low heat for 5 minutes or until heated throughout. Serve with mixed salad.

Mackerel in Foil

2 small mackerel (approx 8 oz. each)
½ teaspoon salt
Freshly ground black pepper
4 oz. tomatoes
½ lemon, thinly sliced
Parsley for garnish
Serves 2

Gut and clean the fish. Do not remove head or tail. Season well with salt and pepper and lay fish on a piece of aluminium foil. Skin the tomatoes and arrange alternate slices of tomato and lemon along fish. Fold up the foil and seal into neat parcel. Place on a baking sheet and bake in the middle of a moderate oven (350°F or Mark 4) for 25 − 30 minutes. Garnish each fish with a sprig of parsley.

Mackerel Rosemary

2 lb. fresh mackerel fillets

Salt

$\frac{1}{4}$ teaspoon garlic powder

4 oz. peeled mushrooms, finely chopped

2 tablespoons skimmed milk powder

$\frac{1}{4}$ teaspoon rosemary

$\frac{1}{4}$ teaspoon onion powder

Large pinch of pepper

1 tablespoon water

1 tablespoon lemon juice

Serves 4

Sprinkle fish with salt and garlic powder. Place in foil-lined baking tin. Mix mushrooms with milk powder, rosemary, onion powder, about $\frac{1}{2}$ teaspoon salt, pepper, water and lemon juice. Spread over fish fillets. Bake in a fairly hot oven (400°F or Mark 6) for 10 to 15 minutes or until fish flakes easily with a fork.

Cod Steak Toledo

2 oz. skinned tomatoes

2 oz. button mushrooms, left whole and washed

2 oz. chopped onion

$\frac{1}{4}$ teaspoon salt

Freshly ground black pepper, to taste

8 oz. cod steak

Parsley

Serves 1

Chop tomatoes, and mix with mushrooms, onion and seasoning. Stand fish on a large square of aluminium foil and place in a fireproof dish. Pile tomato mixture on top and fold over foil to form a parcel. Cook in the middle of the oven at 400°F or Mark 6 for about 30 minutes. Just before serving, open up foil parcel and sprinkle with chopped parsley. Serve with any No. 3 vegetable, such as marrow or courgettes.

Cod Exotic

4 oz. sliced mushrooms

2 teaspoons dried onion flakes

1 teaspoon parsley, chopped

1 lb. cod fillet

1 teaspoon pepper

2 teaspoons wine vinegar

$\frac{1}{4}$ pint chicken stock

2 lemon curls

1 bunch watercress

Serves 2

Combine mushrooms, onion flakes and parsley in a baking dish. Place fish over mixture and season well. Stir wine vinegar into stock and pour over fish. Cover tightly. Bake in a moderate oven at 350°F or Mark 4 for 25 minutes. After this time, remove fish and vegetables and place to one side. Pour fish stock into a small saucepan and reduce quantity by half. Return fish and mushroom mixture to baking dish and pour reduced sauce over. Then, with a fork, lightly break up the flesh into mouth-sized portions and mix with the sauce. Decorate with lemon curls. For extra colour add little sprigs of watercress.

Quickie Fish Cakes

1 teaspoon dried onion flakes

$\frac{1}{4}$ teaspoon Tabasco

$\frac{1}{2}$ teaspoon Worcestershire sauce

$\frac{1}{2}$ teaspoon soy sauce

6 oz. cooked flaked hake

3 teaspoons prepared mustard

1 teaspoon finely chopped parsley

Salt to taste

Serves 1

Combine first 4 ingredients. Let stand about 15 minutes for onions to soften. Add rest of ingredients and mix well. Shape into 2 cakes and brown on both sides in non-stick pan.

69

Mackerel in Foil

Cod Exotic

Cod Steak Toledo

Cod Kebabs

1 lb. thick cod, skinned

1 small green pepper, chopped into 1-inch cubes

4 oz. button onions, peeled

4 oz. tomatoes

4 button mushrooms

4 small bay leaves

Lemon juice

Salt and freshly ground black pepper

$\frac{1}{4}$ level teaspoon paprika

Chopped parsley

Serves 2

Cut the fish into large cubes and cook with green pepper and onions in a pan of water for 5 minutes. Drain. Quarter the tomatoes. Put fish cubes, vegetables and bay leaves onto skewers and brush with lemon juice, season with salt and pepper, and grill under a moderate heat for about 8 minutes. Turn carefully and brush with more lemon juice. Re-season. Sprinkle with chopped parsley and serve with green salad.

Fish Piquant

8 oz. cod or haddock fillet

2 oz. onion

2 oz. skinned tomatoes

1 small green pepper

About 3 drops artificial liquid sweetener

Garlic salt to taste

1 dessertspoon Worcestershire sauce

3 dessertspoons water

2 small bay leaves

Serves 1

Put fish into small heat-proof dish. Chop onion, tomatoes and green pepper finely. Mix with sweetener and garlic salt. Combine Worcestershire sauce and water. Spoon vegetable mixture over fish. Moisten with sauce and water. Stand bay leaves on top. Cover with foil and bake in a moderate oven (350°F or Mark 4) for 35 to 45 minutes according to thickness of fish.

Cod Kebabs

Baked Haddock in Sauce

1 lb. fresh haddock
1 teaspoon salt
1 tablespoon lemon juice
1 tablespoon dried onion flakes
1 tablespoon paprika
2 – 3 drops Tabasco sauce
$\frac{1}{4}$ pint skimmed milk
Serves 2

Place fish in baking pan and sprinkle with salt and lemon juice. Bake in fairly hot oven (400°F or Mark 6) for 15 minutes. Combine onion flakes, paprika, Tabasco sauce and skimmed milk. Pour over fish. Bake an additional 5 minutes or until fish flakes easily with fork.

Poached Haddock with Salmon

12 oz. fresh haddock
4 oz. tinned salmon
For court bouillon:
1 pint water
1 bay leaf
3 teaspoons salt
3 whole peppercorns
1 tablespoon vinegar
Serves 2

Sprinkle haddock with salt. Leave 15 minutes. Rinse, wrap in piece of muslin and place in boiling Court Bouillon. Place lid on saucepan and, when water comes to the boil, turn off heat. Let fish stand covered for about 15 minutes. Drain fish on kitchen paper. Weigh and make up to 6 oz. allowance with salmon. Spread salmon on top of haddock. Serve with peas and No. 3 vegetable.

72

Whiting with French Mustard Sauce

8 oz. whiting, filleted
Salt and pepper
4 oz. onions
1 level tablespoon French mustard
4 tablespoons wine vinegar
Juice of $\frac{1}{2}$ lemon
1 tablespoon finely chopped parsley
Sprigs of parsley to garnish
Serves 1

Arrange fish in heatproof dish and season with salt and pepper. Chop onions finely and sprinkle over fish. Blend together the mustard and vinegar and pour over the fish. Cover and cook in a moderate oven (350°F or Mark 4) for about 20 minutes or until fish flakes easily with a fork. Pour cooking liquid into a saucepan. Stir in lemon juice and boil fairly briskly for about 3 minutes stirring all the time to reduce liquid slightly. Stir in parsley and pour sauce over fish. Garnish with parsley sprigs.

Norwegian Fish Salad

$1\frac{1}{2}$ lb. cooked, flaked white fish

1 tablespoon prepared mustard

2 celery stalks, chopped

4 tablespoons chicken stock

1 tablespoon horseradish, freshly grated

4 tablespoons finely chopped watercress

1 box of mustard and cress, wash
and cut off half the stems

1 red pepper (from a tin) chopped

1 tablespoon cider vinegar

4 large spinach leaves

Serves 4

Combine all ingredients except for the spinach leaves. Toss lightly, then pile onto spinach leaves. Chill before serving.

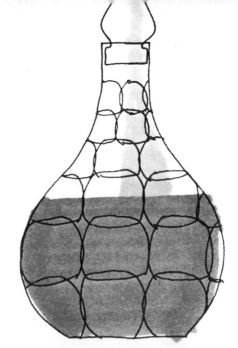

Halibut Special

$\frac{1}{4}$ teaspoon ground mace

$\frac{1}{2}$ teaspoon mixed sweet herbs

$\frac{1}{4}$ pint skimmed milk

2 × 8 oz. halibut steaks

Serves 2

Combine mace, herbs and skimmed milk. Pour over fish in baking dish. Bake in a fairly hot oven (400°F or Mark 6) for about 15 minutes or until fish flakes easily with a fork.

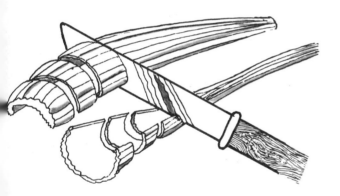

Baked Garlic White Fish

2 lb. white fish fillets

$\frac{1}{4}$ pint chicken stock

1 teaspoon salt

1 tablespoon chopped parsley

2 garlic cloves, minced or very finely chopped

2 teaspoons lemon juice

Serves 4

Baked Lemon Sole

2 lb. fresh lemon sole fillets

2 tablespoons lemon juice

2 tablespoons salt

$\frac{1}{4}$ teaspoon white pepper

1 tablespoon grated orange rind

2 teaspoons grated lemon rind

Serves 4

Sprinkle fish with salt. Stand in baking tin. Combine stock, salt, parsley, garlic and lemon juice. Spoon over fish. Bake at 400°F or Mark 6 for 10 to 20 minutes depending on thickness of fish.

Brush sole with lemon juice. Sprinkle both sides of fish with salt and pepper. Place in baking pan. Sprinkle with citrus rinds. Bake in fairly hot oven (400°F or Mark 6) for 10 minutes or until fish flakes easily with a fork.

73

Norwegian Fish Salad

Mushroom Stuffed Fish

Opposite:
Weight Watchers Dry Fry
74

Mushroom Stuffed Fish

2 oz. button mushrooms
1 oz. tomato, skinned
1 oz. onion
Salt and pepper to taste
Pinch of mixed herbs
1 dessertspoon chopped parsley
8 oz. plaice fillets
Garnish:
2 oz. cooked peas
Serves 1

Chop mushrooms coarsely. Chop tomato and onion finely. Combine vegetables with salt and pepper, mixed herbs and parsley. Place fish in foil-lined baking dish and top with vegetable mixture. Cover and cook in fairly hot oven (400°F or Mark 6) for 20 minutes. Serve with peas.

Weight Watchers Dry Fry

8 oz. rump or fillet steak
2 oz. tomato, skinned and cut in wedges
2 oz. onion, sliced in rings and blanched
2 oz. celery, cut in thin strips
2 oz. tinned red peppers
Salt and pepper
Chopped parsley
Celery tops for garnish
Serves 1

Cube steak and slice vegetables coarsely. Toss all in hot non-stick pan. Cook 3 to 5 minutes, stirring all the time. Season with salt and pepper and sprinkle with parsley. Serve straight away, garnish with celery tops.

Madras Beef Curry

4 oz. onion

1 garlic clove

8 oz. raw, lean stewing steak

1 heaped teaspoon curry powder

*¼ teaspoon Garam Masala
(obtainable at Indian grocers)*

1 green pepper, thinly sliced

6 tablespoons tomato juice

1 teaspoon Worcestershire sauce

Artificial sweetener

¼ pint and 2 tablespoons beef stock

Salt

Serves 1

Brown the onions in a heated non-stick pan with crushed garlic. Add the meat, cut into dice, and brown. Stir in the curry powder and Garam Masala. Turn into casserole and add the sliced green pepper, tomato juice, Worcestershire sauce, sweetener, stock and salt. Cook, covered, in the centre of a warm oven (325°F or Mark 3) for 2½ to 3 hours. Serve with sprigs of cooked cauliflower or bean sprouts.

Spring Thyme Mince

8 oz. lean minced beef

½ teaspoon dried thyme

1 dessertspoon dried onion flakes

1 teaspoon lemon juice

2 teaspoons curry powder

About ½ pint tomato juice

Serves 1

Heat a heavy based pan until very hot, then add the mince, stirring until it browns. Pour off any fat and check weight. Add thyme, onion, lemon juice and curry powder and just cover with tomato juice. Simmer for 20 minutes, adding more juice if necessary. This is very good with carrots or peas and a green vegetable, or it can also be used as a filling for marrow or green peppers.

Sweet and Sour Liver

12 oz. tomato juice

¼ fresh pineapple, cubed

1 teaspoon dried onion flakes

1 tablespoon vinegar

2 teaspoons soy sauce

*Artificial sweetener to equal 4 teaspoons sugar,
or to taste*

1 beef stock cube

½ green pepper, medium diced

8 oz. liver, sliced ¼-inch thick

Serves 1

Combine all ingredients, except liver, in a saucepan. Simmer uncovered for 20 minutes. Add liver and cook 5 to 7 minutes. (Do not overcook).

Weight Watchers "Shepherds Pie"

1 small cauliflower

6 oz. lean cooked lamb, minced

¼ pint tomato juice

4 tablespoons water

1 beef stock cube

1½ teaspoons dried onion flakes

1½ teaspoons dried pepper flakes

1½ teaspoons dried celery flakes

Salt and pepper to taste

1 teaspoon mixed herbs

Paprika

Serves 1

Cook cauliflower in boiling salted water until tender. Drain and mash finely. Put all remaining ingredients (except paprika) into a saucepan. Bring slowly to the boil. Cover and boil gently for 15 minutes. Transfer to a heatproof dish, top with mashed cauliflower and sprinkle with paprika. Reheat in a fairly hot oven (400°F or Mark 6) for 15 minutes.

Liver and Apple Casserole

1 teaspoon dried onion flakes

2 oz. cooking apple, sliced

8 oz. lambs liver, sliced

Salt and pepper

$\frac{1}{2}$ pint tomato juice

4 oz. tomatoes

Serves 1

Place onion flakes in casserole. Top with half the apple slices. Cover with liver, seasoned with salt and pepper. Add remaining sliced apple then pour tomato juice into dish. Cover and bake at 350°F or Mark 4 for 30 minutes. Uncover, place sliced tomato on top and cook for a further 5 minutes.

Liver Kebabs

8 oz. lambs liver

2 oz. onions

2 oz. tomatoes

2 oz. mushrooms

2 oz. green peppers

Marinade:

1 tablespoon of wine or malt vinegar

3 tablespoons tomato juice

Salt and pepper to taste

Serves 1

Cut liver into cubes, place in marinade and cover. Leave in the refrigerator or a cool place for 2 hours. Remove liver and place on skewers with alternate pieces of onion, tomato, mushrooms and pepper. Grill for about 20 minutes, basting occasionally with remaining marinade. Serve with green salad or any green vegetable as desired.

Liver Baked in Foil

8 oz. lambs liver

2 oz. onion, very thinly sliced

Salt and pepper

Mixed herbs

2 oz. skinned and sliced tomato

4 sliced mushrooms

2 tablespoons stock

Serves 1

Thinly slice liver. Place sliced onion on large sheet of aluminium foil. Sprinkle with salt, pepper and herbs. Place liver on top. Cover with tomato and mushrooms. Sprinkle with more salt and pepper and the stock. Wrap up parcel-fashion and stand in a baking tin. Cook in a fairly hot oven (400°F or Mark 6) for 30 minutes. Serve with cauliflower or any No. 3 vegetable.

Liver Italienne

$\frac{1}{4}$ pint tomato juice

1 chicken stock cube

8 oz. calves liver, sliced

2 oz. mushrooms, chopped

1 celery stalk, chopped

1 oz. onion, chopped

$1\frac{1}{2}$ oz. frozen peas

$1\frac{1}{2}$ oz. diced tinned carrots

$\frac{1}{2}$ teaspoon mixed herbs

Serves 1

Heat tomato juice in saucepan. Crumble in stock cube. Add liver, mushrooms, celery and herbs. Cover and simmer for 10 minutes, stirring occasionally. Cook peas, onion and carrots separately. Drain and add to main dish before serving.

Roast Pheasant
(with Festive Fruit Sauce)

1 pheasant

Seasoning

Chicken stock, made from bouillon cube

4 tangerines

4 cooking apples

Artificial sweetener to taste

Water

Lemon juice (optional)

Serves 2

Spring Thyme Mince

**Opposite: Frankfurters
in Tomato Sauce**

Prepare bird and season inside and out. Roast in fairly hot oven (400°F or Mark 6) for about 40 minutes according to size of bird. Baste with stock to keep bird from drying. When cooked, decorate bird with sections of tangerines and one apple. Serve hot with fruit sauce. To make sauce, peel and core rest of apples and stew gently in water. Add sweetener to taste. Then puree fruit through coarse sieve. Add lemon juice if desired.

Veal Roll

1½ lb. veal, finely minced

6 oz. tinned celery

2 oz. peeled and chopped mushrooms

1½ teaspoons salt

¼ teaspoon pepper

2 tablespoons chopped peppers

3 – 4 teaspoons dried onion flakes

Paprika

Serves 3

Mix together veal, celery, mushrooms, salt, pepper and peppers. Soak dried onion flakes in a little hot water for 5 minutes. Drain and add to meat mixture. Shape into a roll and stand on foil-covered baking sheet. Bake in a moderate oven (350°F or Mark 4) for 1 hour.

Frankfurters in Tomato
Sauce

1 tablespoon dried onion flakes

1 small tin (3 oz.) mushrooms, drained

1 green pepper, cut into 1-inch strips

12 fl. oz. tomato juice

½ teaspoon mixed herbs

*Dash each of garlic powder, celery, salt,
parsley flakes, thyme*

Salt and pepper to taste

8 oz. all-beef frankfurters

4 oz. peas and carrots

Serves 1

Combine all ingredients except frankfurters, peas and carrots. Simmer for 20 minutes. Cut frankfurters into 1-inch pieces and grill on a rack until golden brown. Add frankfurters, peas and carrots to tomato juice mixture and simmer for 5 minutes.

78

Chicken Special

4 × 10 oz. chicken joints, skinned

Salt and pepper

½ lb. button mushrooms, wiped with damp cloth and sliced

3 tablespoons dried onion flakes

2 celery stalks, sliced

2 sprigs parsley

2 bay leaves

2 cloves garlic, peeled and chopped

¾ pint chicken stock

Chopped parsley

Serves 4

Split each chicken joint in two. Sprinkle with salt and pepper, brown in a non-stick pan over a medium heat. Transfer to a casserole with lid. Bake at 350°F or Mark 4 for 35 minutes. Meanwhile combine mushrooms, onion flakes, celery, parsley, bay leaves, garlic and stock in a saucepan and bring to the boil. Cover with lid and cook for 30 minutes. Discard parsley and bay leaves. Reduce vegetable juice by half and re-season if necessary. Drain chicken joints, spoon vegetable sauce over them and serve sprinkled with chopped parsley. Serve with peas and a green salad.

Sweet Sour Chicken

2 dessertspoons lemon juice

2 dessertspoons soy sauce

6 dessertspoons water

Artificial sweetener to taste

10 oz. portion chicken joint

2 oz. mushrooms, sliced

Serves 1

Combine first 4 ingredients well together. Skin chicken and put into an ovenproof dish. Cover with lemon juice mixture. Refrigerate, covered, for about 2 hours. Keep covered and cook in centre of warm oven (325°F or Mark 3) for 1¼ hours. Un-cover, top with mushroom slices and continue to cook for a further 15 minutes, basting frequently.

Tomato Chicken Bake

4 level tablespoons dried onion flakes

4 oz. button mushrooms, wiped with damp cloth and sliced

2 tablespoons celery, chopped

4 oz. tin peppers, drained

1 clove garlic, peeled and chopped

Good pinch dried rosemary

Pinch allspice

14 fl. oz. tin tomato juice

1 tablespoon lemon juice

4 × 10 oz. chicken joints, skinned

Salt and freshly ground pepper

Serves 4

Combine onion flakes, mushrooms, celery, 2 tablespoons chopped peppers, garlic, rosemary, allspice and tomato juice. Cook uncovered over medium heat until tomato juice is reduced by half. Stir in lemon juice. Split each chicken joint into two. Sprinkle lightly with salt and pepper. Brown over a medium heat in non-stick pan, turning frequently. Transfer chicken to an oven-proof casserole. Spoon tomato sauce over each chicken portion. Bake in the oven at 325°F or Mark 3 for 35 minutes or until chicken is cooked. Spoon sauce over chicken at intervals of 10 minutes during baking. Garnish with remains of peppers cut into strips and watercress.

Jellied Chicken

1 envelope gelatine
½ pint chicken stock
¼ pint skimmed milk
1 tablespoon lemon juice
½ teaspoon finely grated lemon peel
¾ teaspoon salt
Dash of white pepper
12 oz. cooked diced chicken
½ diced cucumber
1 tablespoon finely chopped parsley
2 chopped pickled cucumbers
Serves 2

Add gelatine to stock and stand over a low heat until gelatine dissolves. Remove from heat and cool to lukewarm. Stir in milk, lemon juice and peel, salt and pepper. Leave to cool until just beginning to thicken and set. Fold in remaining ingredients and transfer to a 2-pint mould, first rinse with cold water. Refrigerate until firmly set and then unmould on to a serving plate. Garnish with salad greens.

Austrian Peppers

8 oz. chicken livers
1 oz. grated onion
1 teaspoon oregano
Salt and pepper to taste
2 medium-sized green peppers
12 fl. oz. tomato juice
Serves 1

Cook livers in water for 10 minutes. Drain and chop finely. Add onion and oregano and season to taste with salt and pepper. Chop tops off peppers (put tops to one side) and remove seeds. Then wash, drain, and fill the peppers tightly with liver mixture. Replace tops. Transfer peppers to saucepan and add tomato juice and ¼ pint water. Cover and simmer for 1 hour, turning occasionally until peppers are light green.

Braised Chicken in Foil

1 chicken leg (approx. 10 oz.)
2 oz. onion
2 oz. tomatoes
2 oz. mushrooms
Salt and pepper to taste
Serves 1

Skin chicken leg and remove surplus fat. Slice onion, tomatoes and mushrooms on to a piece of aluminium foil. Place chicken leg on vegetables and season to taste with salt and pepper. Wrap up tightly and cook in a moderate oven (350°F or Mark 4) for about 1 hour or until chicken is tender. Serve hot with No. 3 vegetables.

Baked Aubergines

1 or 2 aubergines (to weigh 1 lb.)
2 teaspoons dried onion flakes
1 teaspoon mixed herbs
Salt and pepper
Serves 4

Wash aubergines and wrap in foil. Bake in a moderate oven (350°F or Mark 4) for ½ to 1 hour, according to size, until tender. Halve and scoop out centres. Mix this pulp with onion flakes, herbs and seasoning. Return to shells and reheat in oven for 5 – 10 minutes.

Braised Leeks

1 lb. leeks

1 chicken stock cube

½ pint hot water

Serves 4

Wash and prepare leeks. Dissolve cube in hot water. Pour over leeks and bake at 350°F or Mark 4 for 1 hour. Drain liquid before serving.

Chicken Special

Opposite: Tomato Chicken Bake

Sprouts with Celery

4 oz. sprouts

3 stalks celery, chopped

Celery salt and pepper

Serves 1

Prepare sprouts and cook for 15 minutes. Seven minutes before they are ready, add celery. Drain. Serve sprinkled with celery salt and pepper.

Baked Marrow Savoury

1 small marrow

4 oz. onion, grated

1 heaped tablespoon chopped parsley

¼ pint tomato juice

1 dessertspoon Worcestershire sauce

1 teaspoon salt

Black pepper

Serves 1

Cut marrow into cubes and put into heatproof dish. Sprinkle onion over marrow with parsley. Beat tomato juice with remaining ingredients and pour into dish over marrow. Cover and cook in centre of oven (350°F or Mark 4) for 35 to 40 minutes.

Curried Parsnips

4 oz. parsnips

Curry powder

¼ pint chicken stock

1 heaped tablespoon chopped parsley

Serves 1

Peel parsnips and cut into fairly thin slices. Put into a heatproof dish and sprinkle with curry powder and parsley. Pour stock into dish. Cover with lid or foil and bake in centre of moderate oven (350°F or Mark 4) for about 35 to 40 minutes.

Spiced Beetroot

4 oz. cooked beetroot

2 tablespoons cider vinegar

1 bay leaf

1 teaspoon pickling spice

¼ teaspoon salt

Pepper to taste

Serves 1

Slice beetroot thinly and put into a dish. Put all remaining ingredients into a small saucepan and bring to the boil. Strain over beetroot. Serve immediately, or chill first.

Artichokes in Tomato Jelly

1 envelope gelatine (to set 1 pint)

14 fl. oz. tomato juice

1 tablespoon Worcestershire sauce

½ teaspoon onion salt

½ teaspoon peeled and finely grated horse-radish

16 oz. tin artichoke hearts, well drained and quartered

Salt and pepper to taste

4 lemon slices

Parsley sprigs

Serves 4

Combine gelatine and 2 tablespoons tomato juice and stir over a low heat until gelatine dissolves. Stir in the remaining tomato juice. Worcestershire sauce, onion salt, horse-radish, salt and pepper to taste. Chill until just beginning to set. Fold in artichoke hearts and divide jelly between 4 wine glasses. Chill until firm, decorate each with a twist of lemon and sprig of parsley.

Artichokes Citrus

1 tablespoon dried onion flakes

1 clove garlic, sliced

½ pint chicken stock

8 oz. tinned artichoke hearts

2 tablespoons fresh lemon juice

½ teaspoon salt

½ teaspoon marjoram

½ teaspoon basil

Serves 2

Cook onion flakes and garlic in chicken stock for 5 minutes. Add artichoke hearts, lemon juice, salt, marjoram and basil. Simmer gently until heated through. Drain. Serve.

Tomato Platter

3 oz. tomatoes

1 oz. onion

1 tablespoon cider vinegar

1 teaspoon basil

1 tablespoon chopped parsley

½ teaspoon made mustard

Rind of ½ lemon

Salt

Ground black pepper

Artificial sweetener to taste

Serves 1

Cover tomatoes with boiling water. Leave 1 minute, rinse under cold water and gently peel off skins. Slice thinly and arrange on a platter. Slice onion thinly into rings. Place on top of salad. Beat remaining ingredients together and pour over salad.

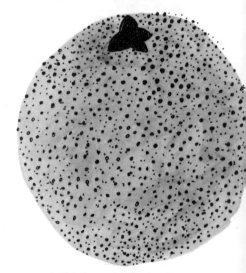

Orange and Chicory Salad

Dressing:

2 tablespoons lemon juice

1 tablespoon water

1 teaspoon curry powder

2 – 3 drops liquid artificial sweetener

Serves 1

Mix 1 peeled and chopped orange with 3 pieces chopped chicory and mix with above dressing.

Peking Salad

4 oz. tinned bamboo shoots, sliced into fine shreds

6 radishes, sliced

4 teaspoons chopped watercress

1 red pepper, cut into fine shreds

2 tablespoons cider vinegar

$\frac{1}{4}$ teaspoon onion salt

$\frac{1}{2}$ teaspoon mixed herbs

2 heaped tablespoons chopped parsley

Salt

Ground black pepper

Artificial sweetener to taste

1 oz. mustard and cress for garnish

Serves 1

Mix all ingredients well together and chill before serving. Place in dish and garnish with a little chopped mustard and cress.

Spiced Vegetable Stew

8 oz. pickled cucumbers, finely chopped

8 oz. cooked green beans, sliced

1 tin (approximately 8 oz.) mushrooms

$\frac{1}{4}$ teaspoon caraway seeds

$\frac{1}{4}$ pint plus 4 tablespoons tomato juice

$\frac{1}{2}$ teaspoon garlic salt (or to taste)

$\frac{1}{2}$ teaspoon onion salt (or to taste)

Serves 3

Combine all ingredients in saucepan. Simmer, covered, for about 10 minutes. Leave overnight, if possible, to improve flavour.

Evening Salad

Raw tomato, raw small onion, raw carrot — to weigh 4 oz. in total

White cabbage

$\frac{1}{4}$ green pepper

Also:

Pinch of parsley, marjoram, chervil

Salt and pepper

Juice of $\frac{1}{4}$ lemon

1 tablespoon vinegar

Serves 1

Shred all vegetables finely, add herbs and seasoning, and toss well in lemon juice and vinegar. Leave in a covered dish to marinade, preferably for at least 2 hours.

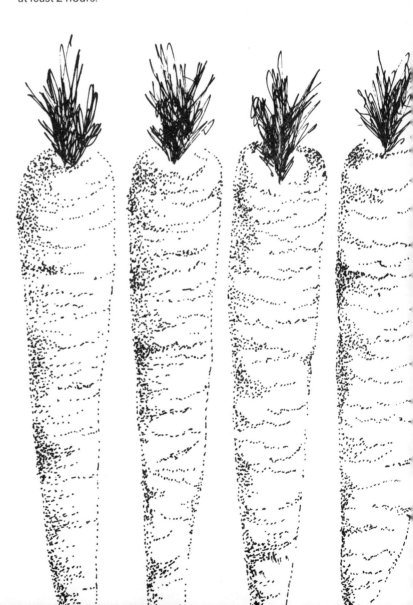

Tomato Platter

Artichokes in Tomato Jelly

Spiced Beetroot

Opposite: Evening Salad

Peking Salad

Orange Strawberry Whip

1 envelope gelatine
4 tablespoons sugar-free orange squash
Finely grated peel of 1 small orange
Cold water
Liquid artificial sweetener to taste
12 oz. strawberries, sliced
Serves 3

Soften gelatine in the squash for 3 minutes. Stand in basin over pan of boiling water and stir until dissolved. Add orange peel, then make up to 1 pint with cold water. Sweeten to taste then cool until just beginning to thicken. Whisk until light and foamy. Stir in sliced strawberries and transfer to a 2-pint mould, first rinsed with cold water. Chill until firm and set.

Strawberry Soufflé

1 envelope gelatine
$\frac{1}{3}$ pint boiling water
$\frac{1}{2}$ pint sugar-free orange squash
1 teaspoon finely grated lemon peel
Cold water
Artificial sweetener to taste
8 oz. fresh strawberries
Serves 2

Dissolve gelatine in the boiling water then stir in squash and lemon peel. Make up to 1 pint with cold water and sweetener to taste. Leave to chill until just beginning to thicken and set. Whisk until light and foamy and spoon into shallow serving bowl. Chill until firm and set. Just before serving, cover top with sliced strawberries.

Strawberry "Cream"

1 envelope gelatine
$\frac{3}{4}$ pint boiling water
8 oz. fresh or frozen strawberries
Finely grated peel of $\frac{1}{2}$ lemon
Juice of 1 lemon
1 tablespoon skimmed milk powder
Artificial sweetener to taste
(to equal 6 teaspoons sugar)
2 drops of cochineal
Serves 2

Dissolve gelatine in boiling water. Cool a little. Put all ingredients into liquidizer (keeping back 2 strawberries for decoration) and blend. Spoon into two bowls or glasses. Place in a refrigerator to set. Decorate with a strawberry in the centre of each.

Tutti Frutti Mix

1 orange
A little cooked rhubarb
2 teaspoons lemon juice
1 tablespoon low-calorie orange squash
A little artificial sweetener
Serves 1

Peel orange with sharp knife, removing all pith. Chop into small pieces. Combine with rhubarb. Add lemon juice and squash. Mix thoroughly and sweeten to taste. Put into a dish and chill.

Stewed Rhubarb — unlimited

2 lb. rhubarb
4 oz. concentrated orange juice (low calorie)
16 drops artificial sweetener (or 4 tablets)
1 teaspoon bicarbonate of soda
$\frac{1}{2}$ pint water (or less if thicker consistency is required)
Serves 4

Cut rhubarb into 1-inch pieces. Put into saucepan with orange squash, water and bicarbonate of soda. Bring to boil slowly and then simmer for approximately 5 to 7 minutes or until rhubarb is soft. Add sweetener to taste. The bicarbonate of soda neutralizes the acid and less sweetener is needed.

Fruit Fool

4 oz. gooseberries, blackberries or black- or redcurrants
$\frac{1}{2}$ oz. skimmed milk powder
3 tablespoons water
Artificial liquid sweetener to equal 3 teaspoons sugar
Serves 1

Top and tail gooseberries and cook in a covered pan with 2 tablespoons water until soft. Blend in liquidizer until smooth then sieve. Add sweetener (and more if necessary). Mix milk powder to a thick cream with 1 tablespoon water and whisk with gooseberry puree. Chill and serve.

Raspberry Tang

4 oz. fresh raspberries
3 teaspoons lemon juice
Artificial sweetener to taste
1 teaspoon finely grated orange peel
Serves 1

Put raspberries into dish. Sprinkle with lemon juice and sweetener to taste. Add orange peel and fold gently into raspberries. Cover. Chill before serving.

Opposite:
Strawberry "Cream"

Strawberry Soufflé

Tutti Frutti Mix

90

Mandarin Soufflé

2 packets powdered gelatine
(6 level teaspoons)
7 fl. oz. low-calorie orange or lemon squash
6 drops artificial liquid sweetener
¼ teaspoonful vanilla essence
1 oz. skimmed milk powder
2 mandarin oranges, satsumas or
clementines, cut into segments
Serves 2 – 3

Place 4 level teaspoons gelatine in a basin with ¼ pint water over a pan of hot water until dissolved. Add undiluted squash and make up to 1 pint with cold water. Chill until set. Dissolve remaining gelatine in 6 fluid oz. water and when dissolved add sweetener and essence. Pour on to the powdered milk and whisk until well mixed. Chill until set. When both are set, first whisk the jelly cream until smooth, then whisk in the other jelly. Fold in the fruit segments and turn into a bowl. Chill for about 15 minutes and serve.

Orange Cocktail

4 oranges
1 lemon
15 – 20 drops artificial sweetener, to taste
8 tablespoons low-calorie orange squash
Serves 4

Peel orange and lemon with sharp knife, removing all pith. Take three of the oranges, cut into small pieces and divide equal amounts between four dishes. Quarter other orange and lemon and place in liquidizer with liquid sweetener and squash. Blend until smooth. Pour over oranges and allow to stand for 2 hours in refrigerator or cool place.

Lemon Ice – unlimited

1 envelope gelatine
6 tablespoons boiling water
Lemon juice to taste (about 5 tablespoons)
Artificial sweetener to taste
½ pint crushed ice
Segments of fresh lemon
Serves 2 – 3

Put gelatine and boiling water into blender on high speed. Blend for 30 seconds. Add lemon juice and artificial sweetener. Cover. When blender blades reach full speed, add crushed ice. Blend 60 seconds. Leave for 2 minutes. Serve in tall glasses decorated with lemon segments.

Vanilla Junket

1¼ pints skimmed milk
1 envelope gelatine
Artificial sweetener to taste
¾ teaspoon vanilla
Serves 4

Soften gelatine in a little of the cold milk. Heat the remaining milk until hot but not boiling. Mix in bowl with gelatine. Add sugar substitute to taste and vanilla. Place in refrigerator until firm.

Coffee Vanilla Cream

2 level teaspoons powdered gelatine
$\frac{1}{2}$ pint cold water
1 oz. skimmed milk powder
2 tablets artificial sweetener
1 level teaspoon instant coffee powder
$\frac{1}{4}$ teaspoon vanilla essence
Serves 2

Dissolve gelatine in 2 tablespoons water in a basin over a pan of hot water. Whisk milk powder, sweetener, coffee powder and essence into remaining water. Stir thoroughly into dissolved gelatine and pour into two wine glasses. Place in refrigerator until set.

Melon Mould

1 envelope gelatine
$\frac{1}{4}$ pint boiling water
$\frac{1}{2}$ pint sugar-free lemon squash
Cold water
Artificial sweetener to taste
4 – inch wedge of honeydew melon,
cut into small cubes
Serves 4

Dissolve gelatine in the boiling water. Add lemon squash then make up to 1 pint with water. Sweeten to taste and cool until just beginning to thicken. Fold in the melon cubes then transfer to a 1$\frac{1}{2}$ to 2 pint fancy mould. Chill until firm and set. Turn out and decorate with fresh mint leaves.

Mock Melon Surprise
— unlimited

1 medium-sized marrow, peeled and cubed
$\frac{1}{2}$ pint sugar-free squash
$\frac{1}{2}$ pint water
1 envelope gelatine
Juice of 1 lemon
Sugar substitute to taste
Serves 4

Cook marrow until tender in squash and water. Drain liquid and make up to 1 pint with more squash to taste. Add gelatine and stir over low heat until dissolved. Add lemon juice. Sweeten to taste. Leave until cold and just beginning to thicken. Fold in marrow then transfer to a 1$\frac{1}{2}$ to 2 pint mould. Chill until firm and set.

ENTERTA

NING

Asparagus Aspic
Hors d'Oeuvre

*1 pint chicken stock made
from bouillon cube*

4 teaspoons gelatine

*8 oz. cooked asparagus tips,
fresh or tinned*

Seasoning to taste

Serves 4

Heat a little of the stock, add gelatine and stir well until dissolved. Add remainder of stock. Season. Allow to cool and thicken. Before quite set, stir in asparagus, saving some tips for decoration. Transfer to four individual moulds and chill until firm. Turn out on to lettuce leaves and decorate each aspic with asparagus tips.

Fondue Chinoise
Main Dish

16 oz. best rump of fillet steak

16 oz. fillet of veal

For bouillon:

4 chicken or beef stock cubes

3 pints water

4 cloves garlic, crushed

Generous pinch of marjoram

Seasoning to taste

Serves 4

Prepare the following sauces:
Sauce Celerie *(see Sauces and Dressings, page 117)*

Horse-radish Tarragon Sauce *(see Sauces and Dressings, page 120)*

Piquant Ketchup *(see Sauces and Dressings, page 117)*

Heat bouillon ingredients in a saucepan and when thoroughly hot transfer to fondue dish. Slice the meat thinly (your butcher may do this for you) and roll. Arrange on a dish in alternate rolls of veal and beef. Put the sauces into individual dishes and arrange around the fondue.

To eat: spear roll of meat with fondue fork, dip into the boiling bouillon and allow to cook for as long or as short a time as liked. When cooked, dip into any of the sauces.

Serve with Tomato Platter *(Dinner Vegetables and Salads, page 84),* accompanied by bowls of unlimited vegetable nibbles such as radishes, cucumber and pickled gherkins.

BERNICE WESTON'S PARTY DINNER

Frozen Orange Cups
Dessert

2 teaspoons gelatine
2 tablespoons boiling water
4 medium-sized oranges
6 tablespoons low-calorie orange squash
Serves 4

Dissolve gelatine in water. Cut tops off oranges and scoop out fruit with a grapefruit knife and a dessertspoon. Puree fruit in liquidizer or pass through a sieve. Add orange squash and dissolved gelatine. Pour into ice tray and put into freezing compartment of refrigerator. After 1 hour mash with a fork. When half frozen, spoon into orange shells. Return to freezing compartment until required. Serve decorated with mint leaves.

Tomato and Beansprout Soup – unlimited

For every two servings allow:
1 pint chicken stock
¼ tin beansprouts, strained
¼ pint tomato juice
Few sprigs cauliflower
1 celery stalk cut into 1-inch pieces
Salt and pepper to taste
¼ teaspoon mixed spice
3 drops artificial sweetener

Put all ingredients, except sweetener, into a saucepan and bring to the boil. Lower heat and cover. Simmer for 1 hour. Add artificial sweetener and serve.

Tomato Jelly

Tomato Jelly

For every four servings allow:
1 envelope gelatine
¾ pint tomato juice
½ teaspoon onion salt
4 lemon wedges
Cucumber slices

Soften gelatine in 3 tablespoons tomato juice. Add 4 more tablespoons tomato juice and pour into saucepan. Stand over low heat, stirring, until gelatine dissolves. Add rest of tomato juice and refrigerate until set in four individual moulds. Turn out on to lettuce leaves. Decorate with cucumber and lemon wedges.

Watercress Soup

Watercress Soup

For each person allow:

1 bunch watercress

½ pint hot water

1 chicken stock cube

1 tablespoon skimmed milk

Ground black pepper

Wash watercress. Roughly chop all but the third, (end part) of stems, which should be thrown away. Dissolve cube in hot water, add watercress and cook for 10 minutes. Remove from heat and liquidize. Add dried skimmed milk and reheat without bringing to the boil. Serve hot or well chilled, decorate with sprigs of watercress.

Bean and Tomato Salad

For each person allow:
1 teaspoon gelatine
1 dessertspoon cold water
5 tablespoons tomato juice, heated
1 oz. cooked, sliced beans
1 teaspoon dried onion flakes
Salt and pepper to taste

Moisten gelatine with cold water. Add hot tomato juice and stir until gelatine dissolves. Add remaining ingredients. Season to taste. Pour into a mould. Serve on lettuce.

Golden Grapefruit

For every two servings allow:
1 grapefruit, halved
Artificial sweetener to taste
$\frac{1}{4}$ level teaspoon powdered cinnamon
Mint leaves to decorate

Pre-heat grill. Loosen flesh from sides of grapefruit and remove pips from centre. Mix together sweetener and cinnamon and spread over grapefruit halves. Grill 4 – 5 minutes or until crisp and bubbly. Decorate with mint leaves.

Orange and Lettuce Salad

For each person allow:
A few long lettuce leaves
1 medium-sized orange
Salt

Finely shred lettuce. Cut orange into small cubes. Toss both together with salt. Serve in tall glass.

Grapefruit Fizz

For each person allow:
$\frac{1}{2}$ grapefruit
Sugar-free tonic water

Squeeze juice from grapefruit and pour into tall glass, topping up with tonic water. This will froth up and look like an ice cream soda.

100

Baked Trout

For each person allow:
1 medium-sized cleaned trout (about 6 oz.)
1 tablespoon lemon juice
2 tablespoons tarragon vinegar
2 tablespoons chicken stock
1 slice toast, cubed
¼ teaspoon salt
Good shake pepper
3 lemon slices
1 teaspoon dried onion flakes
Watercress for garnish

Place trout in shallow ovenproof dish. Sprinkle with lemon juice and vinegar. Cover and stand at room temperature for 2 hours. Combine stock, toast, salt and pepper. Spoon on to fish. Top with lemon slices, then sprinkle with onion flakes. Bake in a fairly hot oven (400°F or Mark 6) for about 25 minutes or until fish flakes easily with a fork. Serve garnished with watercress.

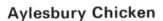

Aylesbury Chicken

For every 4 servings allow:
2 lb. roasting chicken joints
Salt and pepper to taste
1 tablespoon Worcestershire sauce
Juice of 2 large oranges

Skin joints then place in heatproof dish. Sprinkle with salt and pepper then coat with Worcestershire sauce and orange juice. Cover with lid or foil and cook in fairly hot oven (375°F or Mark 5) for 45 minutes to 1 hour, basting once. Serve with any No. 3 vegetable.

Liver with Orange Slices

For each person allow:
6 oz. liver
1 orange
Fresh parsley

Lightly grill liver, then cover with thick slices of orange. Continue cooking until orange slices are hot and liver cooked. Serve sprinkled with chopped parsley and any No. 3 vegetable.

Herb Baked Breast of Veal

1 breast of veal (2 lb.)
1 medium-sized cauliflower
1 tin French green beans, drained and sliced
1 tin mushrooms, drained and diced
¼ pint chicken stock
1 tablespoon soy sauce
Salt and black pepper
4 tablespoons dried onion flakes
2 clove garlic, chopped
⅛ teaspoon thyme
½ bay leaf, chopped
2 sprigs parsley, chopped
2 sprigs rosemary (optional)
½ celery stalk, coarsely chopped
¼ pint cold water
Serves 4

Ask butcher to bone and trim the veal breast and make a pocket in veal. Cook cauliflower and mash well. Preheat oven to 400°F or Mark 6. Combine cauliflower with green beans, mushrooms, salt and pepper and soy sauce. Mix and stuff veal breast. Sew up the opening. Sprinkle with salt and pepper. Place stuffed veal, boned side up, in a lined roasting pan. Scatter onion flakes, garlic, thyme, bay leaf, parsley, rosemary and celery over veal. Reduce heat to 350°F or Mark 4. Cook about 15 minutes. Turn breast to other side. Baste frequently. Cook ¾ hour and pour off fat. Add ¼ pint water and cover with foil. Continue cooking approximately ½ hour longer. Remove foil for last 8 minutes of cooking. Transfer meat to a serving platter. Remove string before slicing veal.

Golden Grapefruit

Herb Baked Breast of Veal
102

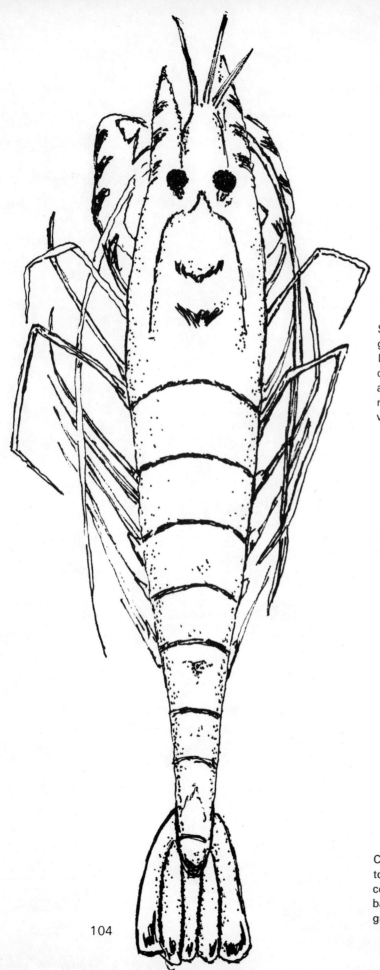

Spiced Roast Sirloin

$3\frac{1}{2}$ lb. sirloin of beef

Salt and pepper

1 teaspoon paprika

2 garlic cloves, crushed

For marinade:

$\frac{1}{2}$ pint water

2 bay leaves

$\frac{1}{2}$ pint vinegar

Serves 6 – 8

Season meat with salt and pepper, paprika and garlic. Marinate meat overnight in refrigerator. Drain. Place meat in a roasting tin. Roast, uncovered, in moderate oven (350°F or Mark 4), allowing about 20 minutes per pound for a medium rare roast. Serve with brussels sprouts (or any No. 4 vegetable).

Shellfish Delight

For each person allow:

$\frac{1}{4}$ pint tomato juice

2 teaspoons oregano

1 celery stalk, chopped

$\frac{1}{2}$ small green pepper, diced

2 teaspoons onion salt

6 oz. cooked scallops, shrimp or crabmeat

Combine all ingredients except fish and cook until tomato juice thickens and mixture is sauce consistency. Add fish and heat through. Serve with baked aubergines (or any No. 4 vegetable) and a green salad.

Plaice Polonaise

For every 2 servings allow:
1 lb. plaice fillets
¼ pint wine or cider vinegar
6 tablespoons water
1 green pepper, seeded and finely diced
1 tablespoon dried onion flakes
¼ teaspoon pepper

Cook plaice in boiling water until JUST tender. Do not overcook or fish may break up. Drain thoroughly, then stand on soft kitchen paper. Combine all remaining ingredients in glass dish. Cut fish into 1-inch squares and add. Cover and refrigerate 24 hours before serving, turning occasionally. Serve with bamboo shoots (or any No. 4 vegetable).

Liver Savoury

For every 4 servings allow:
2 lb. lambs liver, cut into 4 slices
2 teaspoons dried onion flakes
1 teaspoon mixed herbs
2 large apples
Salt and pepper to taste
¾ pint beef stock
Parsley for garnishing

Place liver slices in shallow heatproof dish. Sprinkle with onion flakes and herbs. Peel and core apples and cut into rings. Place on top of liver. Season to taste with salt and pepper then pour stock gently into dish over liver. Cover and bake in moderate oven (350°F or Mark 4) for 1 to 1¼ hours or until liver is tender. Garnish with parsley. Serve with runner beans and any No. 4 vegetable.

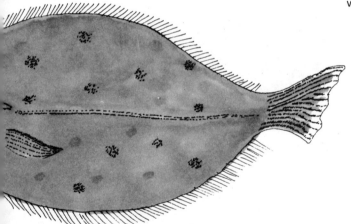

Hong Kong Liver Barbecue

For every 2 servings allow:
6 tablespoons soy sauce
½ teaspoon Aromat
2 slivers fresh ginger root
Artificial sweetener to equal 2 teaspoons sugar
1 lb. sliced lambs liver

Combine all the ingredients except the liver. Pour mixture over the liver and let marinate 4 to 6 hours in the refrigerator. Drain. Grill about 15 minutes, turning frequently. Serve with any No. 4 vegetable.

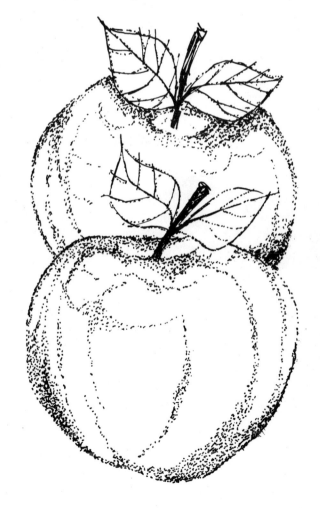

105

Opposite: Apple and Blackcurrant Mousse

Pear Delight

Pear Delight

For every 2 servings allow:

¼ pint low-calorie lemon squash

2 dessert pears, peeled, halved and cored

½ pint skimmed milk

Few strips thinly cut lemon peel

2 teaspoons gelatine

5 tablespoons low-calorie orange squash

*Few drops of liquid sweetener,
(to equal 4 teaspoons of sugar)*

Simmer pears in lemon squash until tender, then drain well, putting to one side ¼ pint of the cooking liquid. Heat milk. Add lemon peel. Then cover and leave to infuse (off heat) for about 30 minutes. Take out peel and throw away. Soak gelatine in the ¼ pint cooking liquid, add to milk and heat gently, stirring to dissolve the gelatine. When dissolved pour in the orange squash. Slice pears into serving dish and pour jelly over them. Leave to set (a thin film of clear jelly will form on top). Decorate with fresh lemon curls, twisted across the top.

Gooseberry and Raspberry Jelly

For every 2 servings allow:

½ lb. gooseberries

½ lb. raspberries

4 tablespoons sugar-free orange squash

Artificial sweetener to taste

1 envelope gelatine

Cold water

Put first 4 ingredients into a saucepan. Simmer gently until fruit is soft. Add gelatine and stir until dissolved. Make up to 1 pint with cold water then turn into a 1½-pint mould, first rinsed with cold water. Refrigerate until firm and set.

108

Rhubarb Mousse

For every 2 servings allow:

1 lb. rhubarb

Low-calorie blackcurrant squash

1 envelope gelatine

1 oz. skimmed milk powder

Artificial sweetener to taste

Cook rhubarb in a little blackcurrant squash. Drain off liquid and place in a measuring jug. Add gelatine and stir until dissolved. Add cooked rhubarb, skimmed milk powder, sweetener to taste and, if necessary, additional squash to bring total contents up to 1 pint. Liquidize at high speed for about 1 minute, pour into dish and allow to set. Remove from refrigerator 1 hour before serving.

Apple and Blackcurrant Mousse

For every 4 servings allow:

1 lb. cooking apples

¼ pint low-calorie blackcurrant squash

½ pint skimmed milk

3 teaspoons powdered gelatine

Peel, core and slice apples. Simmer gently in blackcurrant squash until tender. Liquidize skimmed milk in blender for a few seconds, add apple and blackcurrant while they are still hot and sprinkle in the gelatine. Blend for a further minute. Turn out into 4 individual moulds or glasses and chill.

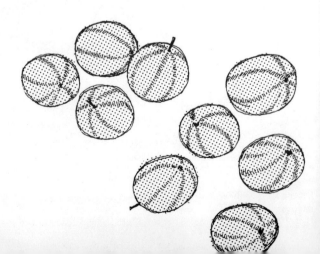

Festive Delight

For each person allow:

4 oz. strawberries or raspberries, frozen or fresh

½ oz. skimmed milk powder

1 tablespoon water

Artificial liquid sweetener, if necessary

Place fruit in the liquidizer and blend till smooth, then pass through a sieve to eliminate seeds. Mix milk powder to a thick cream with 1 tablespoon water and whisk into fruit puree. Chill and serve.

Baked Peaches

For every 2 servings allow:

2 fresh peaches

4 tablespoons sugar-free orange squash

¼ teaspoon ginger

Artificial sweetener to taste

1 teaspoon finely grated orange peel

Peel peaches and slice. Arrange in heatproof dish. Coat with squash then sprinkle with all remaining ingredients. Cover dish and bake in fairly hot oven (400°F or Mark 6) for 20 minutes.

Summer Pear Surprise

For every 4 servings allow:

4 fresh pears

1¼ pints water

Artificial sweetener to equal 4 to 6 oz. sugar

1 teaspoon vanilla extract

8 oz. raspberries

Peel pears. Combine water, sweetener and vanilla in saucepan. Bring to the boil, stirring, until sweetener is dissolved. Add pears. Simmer, covered, 20 minutes or until pears are tender. Cool and drain. Refrigerate until well chilled. Set aside 4 large raspberries. Add remainder to blender. Blend until pureed. Remove from blender. Pour over whole pears. Top each with a raspberry.

109

Cocktail Party Aspics
— unlimited

1 chicken stock cube
1 pint hot water
2 packets (or 6 teaspoons) gelatine
Parsley, chopped
Radishes
Slices of cucumber
Unlimited

Dissolve stock cube in hot water. Allow to cool and skim off fat. Reheat $\frac{1}{4}$ pint stock, add gelatine and stir until dissolved. Add rest of stock, stir well into mix and pour into tin measuring approx. 10"×7"×1". Leave to set hard in refrigerator. Cut into cubes and coat with parsley. Spear a cocktail stick into each cube and serve with radish fans. To make fans, slice base off each radish so that it will stand upright without toppling. Slit two thirds of the way down, then insert half a slice of cucumber into each. Serve immediately.

Pickled Celery — unlimited

1 medium head celery
2 level teaspoons dry mustard
Artificial sweetener to taste
Wine or cider vinegar

Cut washed celery into $\frac{1}{2}$-inch lengths and pack into an empty jar. Mix mustard and sweetener to a smooth paste with a little vinegar. Pour over celery in jar and stir well to mix. Top up jar with more vinegar. Cover and chill for 24 hours before using. Can be served with hot and cold meat or can be eaten on its own as a snack.

110

After Dinner Coffee Lumps

2 teaspoons instant coffee powder
4 tablespoons skimmed milk powder
Artificial sweetener to equal 1 tablespoon sugar
$\frac{1}{2}$ teaspoon vanilla essence
About 3 tablespoons water

Combine first 3 ingredients in small bowl. Sprinkle with essence and water. Stir until mixture forms dry paste that just holds together, adding a little extra skimmed milk powder if necessary. With wet hands, shape mixture into small balls, $\frac{1}{2}$-inch in diameter. Chill in freezer for at least 40 minutes. Makes about 16 balls.

"Fruity" Cubes — unlimited

Vegetable marrow
Low-calorie squash, orange or blackcurrant
Unlimited

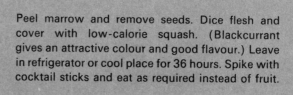

Peel marrow and remove seeds. Dice flesh and cover with low-calorie squash. (Blackcurrant gives an attractive colour and good flavour.) Leave in refrigerator or cool place for 36 hours. Spike with cocktail sticks and eat as required instead of fruit.

Strawberry Lollies

$\frac{1}{4}$ pint plus 4 tablespoons skimmed milk
8 oz. fresh strawberries
Artificial sweetener to equal 2 tablespoons sugar (or more to taste)

Combine skimmed milk and strawberries in blender. Blend at medium speed until mixture is completely smooth. Add sweetener. Blend. Pour into lolly moulds and freeze for about 2 hours or until firm. Before serving, dip lolly moulds into warm water to loosen. Makes 8 lollies, 4 lollies equal 1 fruit allowance.

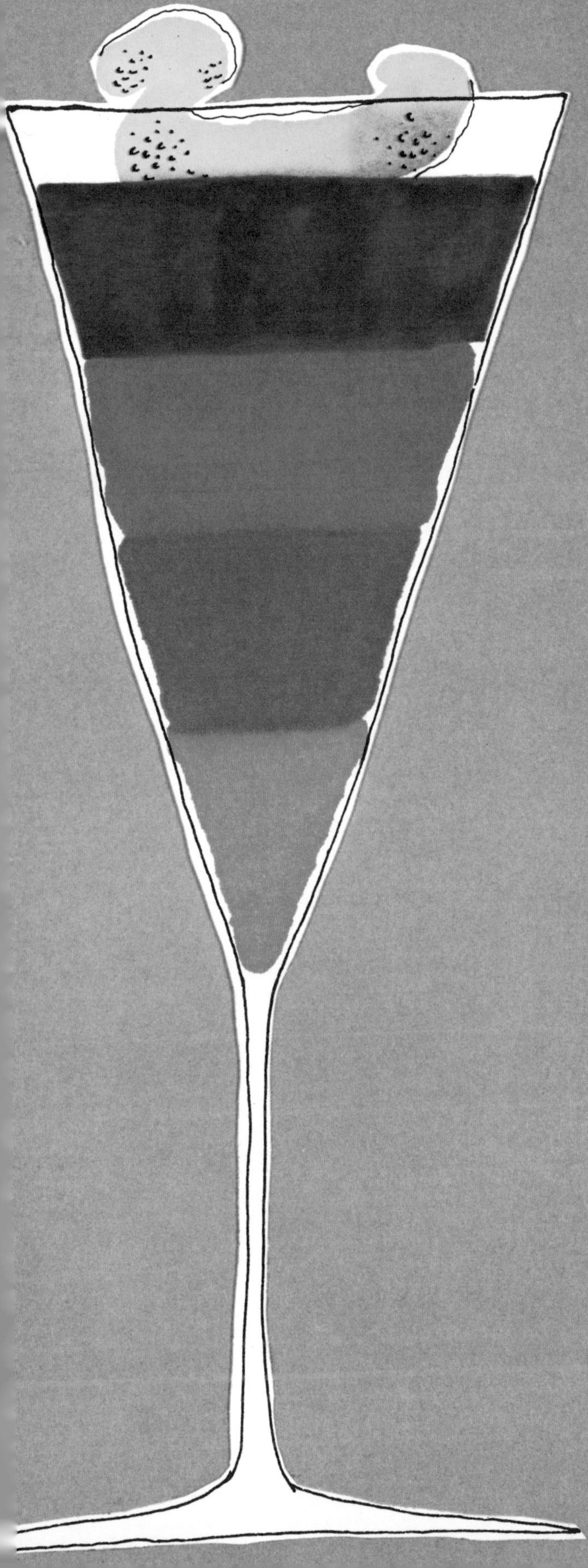

Jamaica Orange
– unlimited

Serves 1

Fill a 6 oz. goblet two-thirds full with Slimline sparkling orange. Add a generous coffeespoonful of rum essence. Serve with ice and a twist of lemon peel.

Mint and Tomato Highball

¼ pint tomato juice

1 teaspoon lemon juice

Dash Worcestershire sauce

6 thin slices cucumber

2 cubes of ice, crushed

2 sprigs of mint – retain one for decoration

Serves 2

Put all ingredients into blender and run at high speed until smooth; about ½ minute. Season to taste with salt or any other desired seasoning. Serve immediately. Decorate with mint leaves. (You can crush ice cubes by wrapping them in a towel, then pounding with a mallet, hammer, rolling pin, etc.)

Contrary Mary

Serves 1

Fill a 6 oz. goblet two-thirds full with tomato juice. Top up with Slimline tonic water. Add a shake of Worcestershire sauce and a good dash of pure lemon juice. A pinch of powdered horse-radish is optional. Stir and serve with ice.

111

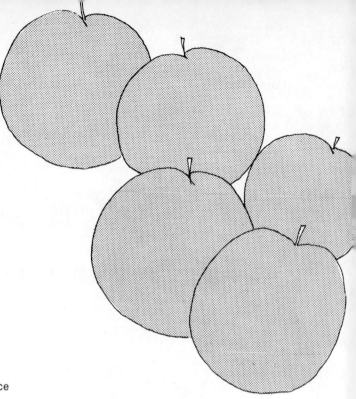

Bloody Shame

$\frac{1}{4}$ *pint tomato juice*

1$\frac{1}{2}$ teaspoons Worcestershire sauce

Dash of pepper

Serves 2

Combine all ingredients. Mix well. Pour over ice cubes in glass. Serve immediately.

Satin Slipper

4 tablespoons low-calorie bitter lemon

6 tablespoons tomato juice

1 teaspoon lemon juice

1 or 2 chopped mint leaves

Serves 1

Combine well-chilled ingredients and serve.

Almond Ginger – unlimited

Serves 1

Fill a 6 oz. goblet two-thirds full with Slimline dry ginger. Add 4 – 5 drops of almond essence. Serve with ice and a sliver of orange.

Cocktail Refresher

$\frac{3}{4}$ *pint tomato juice*

1 small stalk celery, with leaves, diced

2 tablespoons parsley sprigs

2 slices lemon, with peel

1 teaspoon dried onion flakes

$\frac{1}{4}$ *teaspoon salt*

Dash of artificial sweetener (optional)

Serves 4

Mint Dewlip – unlimited

2 tablespoons mint leaves, chopped

Artificial sweetener to equal 1 oz. sugar

1$\frac{1}{2}$ pints Slimline ginger ale

Serves 4

Combine mint leaves and sweetener. Add ginger ale. Let stand at least 30 minutes. Pour over ice cubes in glass and serve immediately.

Put into blender and run at high speed until all vegetables are liquified. Allow to stand 20 minutes before serving in tall glasses.

Apricot Flip

1 lb. fresh apricots

$\frac{1}{4}$ pint water

Artificial sweetener to taste

3 pints skimmed milk

Serves 4

Put apricots, water and sweetener into saucepan. Bring to boil and lower heat. Cover and simmer until apricots are soft. Remove stones then put apricots, liquor from pan and skimmed milk into blender. Blend until frothy. Pour into 4 glasses. Drink straight away.

Iced Coffee Custard

1 envelope unflavoured gelatine

6 tablespoons boiling water

1 oz. skimmed milk powder

1 teaspoon instant coffee powder

1 small capful vanilla extract

6 ice cubes, crushed

Serves 1

Put gelatine in blender. Add boiling water and blend until gelatine is dissolved. Add all other ingredients except ice. Blend until dissolved. Gradually add crushed ice. Allow to stand 5 minutes. Serve in tall glass.

Strawberry Milk Shake

2 oz. skimmed milk powder

4 oz. strawberries

Approx. 16 drops liquid artificial sweetener to taste

About 4 drops vanilla essence

$\frac{1}{2}$ pint cold water

Serves 1

Put all ingredients into blender and blend until smooth. Pour into a large tumbler. Chill. Decorate with twist of fresh orange or fresh strawberry.

113

3 drinks:
Mint Dewlip,
Bloody Shame,
Satin Slipper

SAUCES AND DRESSINGS

Sauce Celerie – unlimited

1 medium head of celery
1 tablespoon dried onion flakes
¾ pint chicken stock
Salt and pepper to taste
Unlimited

Cut celery stalks, with leaves, into 1-inch pieces. Cover with stock in large saucepan. Add onion flakes. Cook uncovered over medium to high heat for about ½ hour until celery is tender and liquid reduced to approximately ½ pint. Pour mixture into blender and blend at low speed until smooth. Season to taste.

Creamed Mushroom Sauce

8 oz. mushrooms, finely chopped
¼ pint chicken stock
2 tablespoons skimmed milk powder
Salt and pepper to taste
Makes about ½ pint

Put mushrooms into a saucepan, add liquid stock and cook for 10 minutes. Stir in dried milk and seasoning to taste.

Piquant Ketchup

1½ pints tomato juice
3 tablespoons dried onion flakes
2 tablespoons Italian seasoning
½ pint cider vinegar
1 teaspoon basil leaves
⅛ teaspoon dill seed
⅛ teaspoon Worcestershire sauce
Makes about ¾ pint

Combine all ingredients in pan. Cook over low heat for 2 hours or until mixture is reduced by half.

117

Weight Watchers Bread Sauce

to serve with chicken

½ pint skimmed milk

Good pinch powdered cloves

Freshly ground pepper

¼ teaspoon salt

1 teaspoon dried onion flakes

4 oz. breadcrumbs

Serves 4

Cook all ingredients except crumbs until onion has softened. Stir in breadcrumbs and mix thoroughly. Cook for 3 – 4 minutes. Add more water as liquid evaporates to keep amount to about ½ pint. Wholemeal bread could be used instead of white to give more contrast against white chicken joints. May only be used to accompany a lunch recipe.

119

Weight Watchers Mayonnaise

1 level tablespoon skimmed milk powder

1 tablespoon cider vinegar

¾ level teaspoon dry mustard

*Artificial liquid sweetener to equal
4 teaspoons sugar*

Salt and pepper

Serves 1

Mix all ingredients together, blending thoroughly. Store in a jar in the refrigerator.

Horse-Radish Tarragon Sauce

2 teaspoons fresh grated horse-radish

1 tablespoon tarragon vinegar

3 tablespoons lemon juice

¼ pint water

Artificial sweetener equal to 1 tablespoon sugar

1 teaspoon salt

1 teaspoon paprika

6 oz. skimmed milk powder

Makes about ¾ pint

Combine all ingredients in electric blender. Blend for about 30 seconds or until thoroughly blended. Chill for about 2 hours. One ounce of dressing equals 3 ounces of liquid skimmed milk.

Weight Watchers Stuffing

4 oz. breadcrumbs

1 tablespoon thyme

3 celery stalks, finely chopped

1 teaspoon lemon peel, finely grated

2 tablespoons dried onion flakes

*1 small green pepper, seeded and
finely chopped*

Skimmed milk for binding

Serves 4

Combine breadcrumbs, thyme, celery, lemon peel, onion flakes and green pepper in small bowl. Bind loosely with skimmed milk and use for chicken or fish.

"Mint Jelly" — unlimited

6 tablespoons wine vinegar

1 envelope gelatine

*10 – 15 drops of artificial sweetener
(according to taste)*

Few drops of green food colouring

2 – 3 tablespoons fresh, chopped mint

Serves 4

Put the wine vinegar into a measuring jug and add gelatine. Top to the 15 fl. oz. mark with boiling water and stir. Add liquid sweetener, colouring and mint. When cool, pour into screw-top jar and leave to set either in a cold larder or refrigerator.

METRIC CONVERSION TABLE

Pounds and Ounces to Kilogrammes and Grammes

1 lb. (16 oz.)	=	454 grammes (little under $\frac{1}{2}$ kilo)
8 oz.	=	227 grammes (little under $\frac{1}{4}$ kilo)
4 oz.	=	113 grammes (little over $\frac{1}{10}$ kilo)
1 oz.	=	28 grammes

Kilogrammes and Grammes to Pounds and Ounces

1 kilo (1000 grammes)	=	2 lb. 3 oz.
$\frac{1}{2}$ kilo	=	1 lb. 1$\frac{1}{2}$ oz.
$\frac{1}{4}$ kilo	=	8$\frac{3}{4}$ oz.
125 grammes	=	4$\frac{3}{8}$ oz.

Pints and Fluid Ounces to Litres and Decilitres

1 pint	=	568 grammes ($\frac{3}{5}$ litre)
$\frac{1}{2}$ pint	=	285 grammes ($\frac{3}{10}$ litre)
$\frac{1}{4}$ pint	=	142 grammes ($\frac{3}{20}$ litre)
1 fluid ounce	=	28 grammes

Litres and Decilitres to Pints and Fluid Ounces

1 litre	=	1$\frac{3}{4}$ pints (35 fluid oz.)
$\frac{1}{2}$ litre	=	$\frac{7}{8}$ pint (17$\frac{1}{2}$ fluid oz.)
$\frac{1}{4}$ litre	=	9 fluid oz.
1 decilitre	=	3$\frac{1}{2}$ fluid oz.

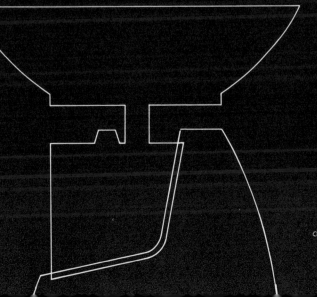

COOKING AND SHOPPING THE WEIGHT WATCHERS WAY

Fish

To Grill: Place fish (either filleted or on bone) on foil, sprinkle generously with lemon juice and seasoning. Place under hot grill and cook until fish flakes easily.

To Casserole: Place fish portion in casserole, cover with tomato juice, liquid skimmed milk, bouillon or lemon juice. Add seasoning and any freely allowed No. 3 vegetables such as mushrooms, courgettes, parsley, pimentos or peppers. Cover and cook until tender.

To Poach: Place fish in pan and cover with salted water. Simmer gently until fish flakes.

To Steam: Put fish on to a plate and place on top of saucepan of boiling water. Sprinkle fish with lemon juice and seasoning, cover with a second plate and cook until fish flakes easily.

Warning : all cooking must be done without fat or oil

Meat and Poultry

All meat juices must be strained before serving. A Weight Watchers gravy or sauce which has been made separately may then be added.

To grill or casserole, follow the same methods as given for fish, see above.

Beef

To Roast: Place beef on rack in roasting tin. Sprinkle with seasoning and soy sauce or Worcestershire sauce if desired. Put a small quantity of water in roasting dish and cook beef in usual way.

Lamb

To Roast: Same method as beef. If desired insert four slivers of garlic into skin of joint and rub 1 teaspoon dry mustard into skin before roasting.

Veal

To Roast: Same method as beef. Use rosemary or other herbs, as desired.

Poultry

To Roast: Place prepared chicken or other allowed poultry on large sheet of foil. Sprinkle with seasoning and herbs (tarragon is especially good with chicken). Wrap foil completely over bird. Place in roasting dish and cook in the usual way.

Liver

To Fry: Heat non-stick pan slowly, then place slices of liver in pan and cook quickly on both sides.

Cooking Utensils

The Weight Watchers Programme of Eating requires you to eat only normal foods, therefore no special equipment is needed for cooking. However, as we do not cook with either fat or oil, a non-stick pan for dry frying will be useful. The following may also come in handy for soups, pâtés, soufflés, puddings etc:
Non-stick saucepan
Liquidizer
Whisk, hand or electric
Rotary grater

Essential : a pair of kitchen scales for weighing exact amounts of food as specified in Programme.

To make Sauce: Remove liver to warm dish. Put into pan either tomato juice or bouillon and add sliced peppers, mushrooms and/or other No. 3 vegetables. Cook until vegetables are tender. Pour over liver and serve.
To Bake: Place unsliced liver on sheet of foil. Sprinkle with mixed herbs and wrap firmly. Bake on a baking dish in moderate oven until tender. To Casserole: As for fish but with either tomato juice, skimmed milk or bouillon.

Vegetables

Mushrooms
To Grill: Wash well. Do not peel button mushrooms. Place on foil. Season. Cook under hot grill turning once during cooking.
Tomatoes
Grill on foil, skin-side first, then reverse side. Sprinkle with 1 or 2 drops of liquid sweetener, herbs or other seasoning.
Onions
Chop and grill on foil with seasoning.

Fruit

Oranges
As a change from fresh fruit, serve grilled orange halves for dessert.
Grapefruit
To make an unusual first course, grill grapefruit halves. Sprinkle with chopped mint and serve.

Shopping

It is in the shops that much "accidental" cheating begins if food is selected carelessly without looking closely at the labels. The net weight of the pack should be checked and, **very important**, the list of ingredients should be thoroughly examined to ensure that no illegal ingredients are included. When buying bread, remember that ordinary bread, white or wholemeal, sliced or unsliced, is what you select. No rolls, no slimming or speciality breads, no crisp breads.
Fruit and vegetables should always be as fresh as possible to ensure best flavour and to make them thoroughly appetizing.
As with tinned foods, all frozen foods are permitted, providing the ingredients are in accordance with the Programme.

Store Cupboard

This may be the source of either failure or success. Ensure it is well stocked with basic foods essential to the Programme, i.e. dried skimmed milk, bouillon cubes, tomato juice, non-flavoured gelatine, low-calorie squashes etc. Otherwise, if you run out of a basic food, you may be tempted to use the illegal equivalent available to the rest of the family. To make selection easy, assemble your food supplies into three groups or shelves. 1. free foods which you can raid willy nilly as the mood takes you; 2. legal but limited foods; 3. illegal foods which are used by the rest of the family, i.e. ketchup, tinned soups. Keep these well out of easy reach.
Keep a wide range of herbs, legal flavourings such as Worcestershire sauce, soy sauce, horse-radish and mustard, and extracts and essences such as peppermint, rum essence and brandy essence.
Learn to enjoy food in its widest sense and find new textures and flavours to replace the old ones which made you fat. Experiment with unfamiliar tastes and make food even more tasty and exciting than before.
Dried herbs make food tasty but home-grown fresh herbs are even better. If you have no garden, grow fresh herbs in a window box. Rosemary, sage and thyme grow very easily and so, too, will bean sprouts (for salads, as a vegetable or as a mock spaghetti).

Refrigerator

Use the refrigerator to keep your food in its most appetizing condition.
Make up bulk amounts of legal Weight Watchers sauces to last you through the week and refrigerate. As they are ready for instant use, you are less likely to be tempted to use the family's illegal sauces. Also bulk-prepare salad dressings and soups. Keep an "Apéritif bowl" in the refrigerator, made up with free vegetables like raw cauliflower, green pepper, celery, radishes, cabbages and cucumber, all chopped and prepared for instant nibbling. An especially good instant nibble is raw button mushrooms, washed, dried and sprinkled with garlic salt.
Texture and colour are every bit as important as taste. When shopping treat yourself to the brightest radishes, the best-looking tomatoes, the fattest asparagus. You can afford them now that you are not buying extravagant, fattening luxuries. Use the refrigerator to keep them in peak condition.

INDEX

125